KB020916

아서와 크런치 시리얼 콘테스트

아서와 크런치 시리얼 콘테스트
(Arthur and the Crunch Cereal Contest)

1판 1쇄 2013년 9월 2일
1판 9쇄 2020년 8월 7일

지은이 Marc Brown
기획 이수영
책임편집 김보경 차소향
콘텐츠제작및감수 롱테일북스 편집부
저작권 김보경
마케팅 김보미 정경훈

펴낸이 이수영
펴낸곳 (주)롱테일북스
출판등록 제2015-000191호
주소 04043 서울특별시 마포구 양화로 12길 16-9 (서교동) 북앤빌딩 3층
전자메일 helper@longtailbooks.co.kr
(학원 · 학교에서 본도서를 교재로 사용하길 원하시는 경우 전자메일로 문의주시면
자세한 안내를 받으실 수 있습니다.)

ISBN 978-89-5605-676-0 14740

롱테일북스는 (주)북하우스 퍼블리셔스의 계열사입니다.

이 도서의 국립중앙도서관 출판시도서목록(CIP)은 서지정보유통지원시스템 홈페이지(http://seoji.nl.go.kr)와
국가자료공동목록시스템(http://www.nl.go.kr/kolisnet)에서 이용하실 수 있습니다. (CIP 제어번호 : CIP 2013013006)

CONTENTS

대한민국 영어 학습자라면 꼭 한번 읽어봐야 할, 아서 챕터북 시리즈!

아서 챕터북 시리즈(Arthur Chapter Book series)는 미국의 작가 마크 브라운(Marc Brown)이 쓴 책입니다. 레이크우드 초등학교에 다니는 주인공 아서(Arthur)가 소소한 일상에서 벌이는 다양한 에피소드를 담은 이 책은, 기본적으로 미국 초등학생들을 위해 쓰인 책이지만 누구나 공감할 만한 재미있는 스토리로 출간된 지 30년이 넘은 지금까지 남녀노소 모두에게 큰 사랑을 받고 있습니다. 아서가 주인공으로 등장하는 이야기는 리더스북과 챕터북 등 다양한 형태로 출판되었는데, 현재 미국에서만 누적 판매 부수가 6천6백만 부를 돌파한 상황으로 대한민국 인구 숫자보다 더 많은 책이 판매된 것을 생각하면 그 인기가 어느 정도 인지 실감할 수 있습니다.

특히 이 『아서 챕터북』은 한국에서 영어 학습자를 위한 최적의 원서로 큰 사랑을 받고 있기도 합니다. 『영어 낭독 훈련』, 『잠수네 영어 학습법』, 『솔빛이네 엄마표 영어연수』 등 많은 영어 학습법 책들에서 『아서 챕터북』을 추천 도서로 선정하고 있으며, 수많은 영어 고수들과 영어 선생님들, '엄마표 영어'를 진행하는 부모님들에게도 반드시 거쳐 가야 하는 영어원서로 전폭적인 지지를 얻고 있습니다.

번역과 단어장이 포함된 워크북, 그리고 오디오북까지 담긴 풀 패키지!

이 책은 이렇게 큰 사랑을 받고 있는 영어원서 『아서 챕터북』 시리즈에, 더욱 탁월한 학습 효과를 거둘 수 있도록 다양한 콘텐츠를 덧붙인 책입니다.

- 영어원서: 본문에 나온 어려운 어휘에 볼드 처리가 되어 있어 단어를 더욱 분명히 인지하며 자연스럽게 암기하게 됩니다.
- 단어장: 원서에 나온 어려운 어휘가 '한영'은 물론 '영영' 의미까지 완벽하게 정리되어 있으며, 반복되는 단어까지 넣어두어 자연스럽게 복습이 되도록 구성했습니다.
- 번역: 영어와 비교할 수 있도록 직역에 가까운 번역을 담았습니다. 원서 읽기에 익숙하지 않는 초보 학습자들도 어려움 없이 내용을 파악할 수 있습니다.
- 퀴즈: 현직 원어민 교사가 만든 이해력 점검 퀴즈가 들어있습니다.
- 오디오북: 미국 현지에서 판매중인 빠른 속도의 오디오북(분당 약 145단어)과

국내에서 녹음된 따라 읽기용 오디오북(분당 약 110단어)을 포함하고 있어 듣기 훈련은 물론 소리 내어 읽기에까지 폭넓게 사용할 수 있습니다.

이 책의 수준과 타깃 독자

- 미국 원어민 기준: 유치원 ~ 초등학교 저학년
- 한국 학습자 기준: 초등학교 저학년 ~ 중학교 1학년
- 영어원서 완독 경험이 없는 초보 영어 학습자 (토익 기준 450~750점대)
- 비슷한 수준의 다른 챕터북: Magic Tree House, Marvin Redpost, Zack Files, Captain Underpants
- 도서 분량: 5,000단어 초반 (약 5,000~5,200단어)

아서 챕터북, 이렇게 읽어보세요!

- **단어 암기는 이렇게!** 처음 리딩을 시작하기 전, 해당 챕터에 나오는 단어들을 눈으로 쭉 훑어봅니다. 모르는 단어는 좀 더 주의 깊게 보되, 손으로 써가면서 완벽하게 암기할 필요는 없습니다. 본문을 읽으면서 이 단어들을 다시 만나게 되는데, 그 과정에서 단어의 쓰임새와 어감을 자연스럽게 익히게 됩니다. 이렇게 책을 읽은 후에, 단어를 다시 한번 복습하세요. 복습할 때는 중요하다고 생각하는 단어들을 손으로 써가면서 꼼꼼하게 외우는 것도 좋습니다. 이런 방식으로 책을 읽다보면, 많은 단어를 빠르고 부담 없이 익히게 됩니다.

- **리딩할 때는 리딩에만 집중하자!** 원서를 읽는 중간 중간 모르는 단어가 나온다고 워크북을 들춰보거나, 곧바로 번역을 찾아보는 것은 매우 좋지 않은 습관입니다. 모르는 단어나 이해가 가지 않는 문장이 나온다고 해도 펜으로 가볍게 표시만 해두고, 전체적인 맥락을 잡아가며 빠르게 읽어나가세요. 리딩을 할 때는 속도에 대한 긴장감을 잃지 않으면서 리딩에만 집중하는 것이 좋습니다. 모르는 단어와 문장은, 리딩이 끝난 후에 한꺼번에 정리해보는 '리뷰'시간을 갖습니다. 리뷰를 할 때는 번역은 물론 단어장과 사전도 꼼꼼하게 확인하면서 왜 이해가 되지 않았는지 확인해 봅니다.

- **번역 활용은 이렇게!** 이해가 가지 않는 문장은 번역을 통해서 그 의미를 파악할

수 있습니다. 하지만 한국어와 영어는 정확히 1:1 대응이 되지 않기 때문에 번역을 활용하는 데에도 지혜가 필요합니다. 의역이 된 부분까지 억지로 의미를 대응해서 암기하려고 하기보다, 어떻게 그런 의미가 만들어진 것인지 추측하면서 번역은 참고자료로 활용하는 것이 좋습니다.

- **듣기 훈련은 이렇게!** 리스닝 실력을 향상시키길 원한다면 오디오북을 적극적으로 활용하세요. 처음에는 오디오북을 틀어놓고 눈으로 해당 내용을 따라 읽으면서 훈련을 하고, 이것이 익숙해지면 오디오북만 틀어놓고 '귀를 통해' 책을 읽어보세요. 눈으로는 한 번도 읽지 않은 책을 귀를 통해 완벽하게 이해할 수 있다면 이후에는 영어 듣기로 고생하는 일은 거의 없을 것입니다.

- **소리 내어 읽고 녹음하자!** 이 책은 특히 소리 내어 읽기(Voice Reading)에 최적화된 문장 길이와 구조를 가지고 있습니다. 또한 오디오북 CD에 포함된 '따라 읽기용' 오디오북으로 소리 내어 읽기 훈련을 함께할 수 있습니다. 소리 내어 읽기를 하면서 내가 읽은 것을 녹음하고 들어보세요! 자신의 영어 발음을 들어보는 것은 몹시 민망한 일이지만, 그 과정을 통해서 의식적 · 무의식적으로 발음을 교정하게 됩니다. 이렇게 영어로 소리를 만들어 본 경험은 이후 탄탄한 스피킹 실력의 밑거름이 될 것입니다.

- **2~3번 반복해서 읽자!** 영어 초보자라면 2~3회 반복해서 읽을 것을 추천합니다. 초보자일수록 처음 읽을 때는 생소한 단어들과 스토리 때문에 내용 파악에 급급할 수밖에 없습니다. 하지만 일단 내용을 파악한 후에 다시 읽으면 어휘와 문장 구조 등 다른 부분까지 관찰하면서 조금 더 깊이 있게 읽을 수 있고, 그 과정에서 리딩 속도도 빨라지고 리딩 실력을 더 확고하게 다지게 됩니다.

- **'시리즈'로 꾸준히 읽자!** 한 작가의 책을 시리즈로 읽는 것 또한 영어 실력 향상에 큰 도움이 됩니다. 같은 등장인물이 다시 나오기 때문에 내용 파악이 더 수월할 뿐 아니라, 작가가 사용하는 어휘와 표현들도 자연스럽게 반복되기 때문에 탁월한 복습 효과까지 얻을 수 있습니다. 『아서 챕터북』 시리즈는 현재 10권, 총 50,000단어 분량이 출간되어 있습니다. 이 책들을 시리즈로 꾸준히 읽으면서 영어 실력을 쑥쑥 향상시켜 보세요!

영어원서 본문 구성

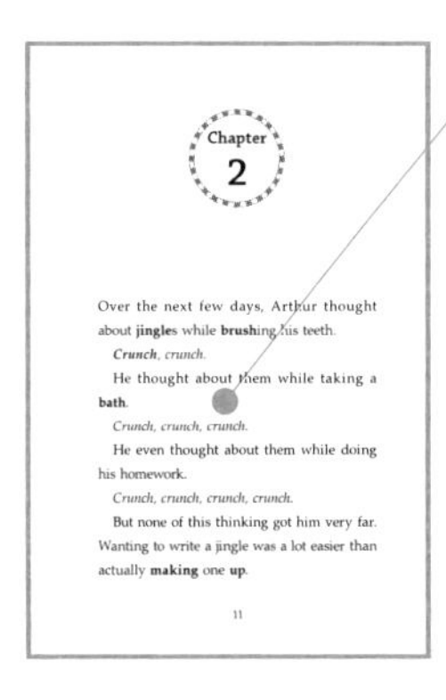

Chapter 2

Over the next few days, Arthur thought about **jingles** while **brushing** his teeth.

Crunch, *crunch*.

He thought about them while taking a **bath**.

Crunch, crunch, crunch.

He even thought about them while doing his homework.

Crunch, crunch, crunch, crunch.

But none of this thinking got him very far. Wanting to write a jingle was a lot easier than actually **making** one **up**.

11

내용이 담긴 본문입니다.

원어민이 읽는 일반 원서와 같은 텍스트지만, 암기해야 할 중요 어휘들은 볼드체로 표시되어 있습니다. 이 어휘들은 지금 들고 계신 워크북에 챕터별로 정리되어 있습니다.

학습 심리학 연구 결과에 따르면, 한 단어씩 따로 외우는 단어 암기는 거의 효과가 없다고 합니다. 대신 단어를 제대로 외우기 위해서는 문맥(Context) 속에서 단어를 암기해야 하며, 한 단어 당 문맥 속에서 15번 이상 마주칠 때 완벽하게 암기할 수 있다고 합니다.

이 책의 본문은 중요 어휘를 볼드로 강조하여, 문맥 속의 단어들을 더 확실히 인지(Word Cognition in Context)하도록 돕고 있습니다. 또한 대부분의 중요한 단어들은 다른 챕터에서도 반복해서 등장하기 때문에 이 책을 읽는 것만으로도 자연스럽게 어휘력을 향상시킬 수 있습니다.

또한 본문에는 내용 이해를 돕기 위해 '각주'가 첨가되어 있습니다. 각주는 굳이 암기할 필요는 없지만, 알아두면 내용을 더 깊이 있게 이해할 수 있어 원서를 읽는 재미가 배가됩니다.

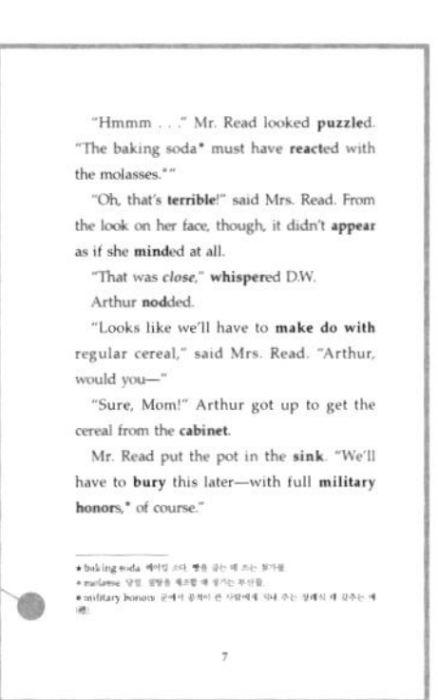

"Hmmm . . ." Mr. Read looked **puzzled**. "The baking soda* must have **reacted** with the molasses.*"

"Oh, that's **terrible**!" said Mrs. Read. From the look on her face, though, it didn't **appear** as if she **minded** at all.

"That was *close*," **whispered** D.W.

Arthur **nodded**.

"Looks like we'll have to **make do with** regular cereal," said Mrs. Read. "Arthur, would you—"

"Sure, Mom!" Arthur got up to get the cereal from the **cabinet**.

Mr. Read put the pot in the **sink**. "We'll have to **bury** this later—with full **military honors**,* of course."

* baking soda [illegible]
* molasses [illegible]
* military honors [illegible]

7

워크북(Workbook)의 구성

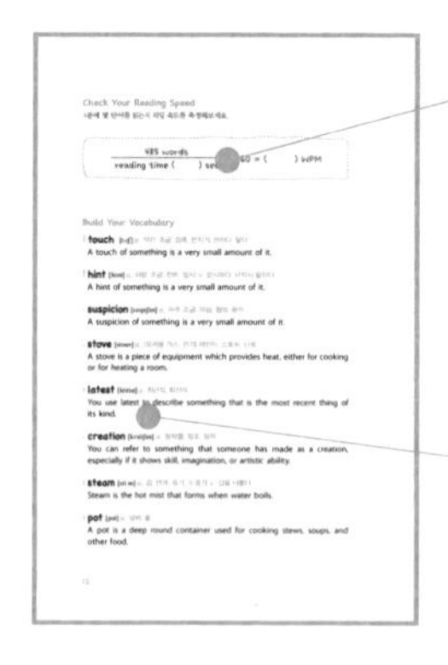
Check Your Reading Speed

485 words / reading time ( ) sec × 60 = ( ) WPM

Build Your Vocabulary

touch
A touch of something is a very small amount of it.

hint
A hint of something is a very small amount of it.

suspicion
A suspicion of something is a very small amount of it.

stove
A stove is a piece of equipment which provides heat, either for cooking or for heating a room.

latest
You use latest to describe something that is the most recent thing of its kind.

creation
You can refer to something that someone has made as a creation, especially if it shows skill, imagination, or artistic ability.

steam
Steam is the hot mist that forms when water boils.

pot
A pot is a deep round container used for cooking stews, soups, and other food.

Check Your Reading Speed

해당 챕터의 단어 수가 기록되어 있어, 리딩 속도를 측정할 수 있습니다. 특히 리딩 속도를 중시하는 독자들이 유용하게 사용할 수 있습니다.

Build Your Vocabulary

본문에 볼드 표시되어 있는 단어들이 정리되어 있습니다. 리딩 전, 후에 반복해서 보면 원서를 더욱 쉽게 읽을 수 있고, 어휘력도 빠르게 향상됩니다.

단어는 〈빈도 – 스펠링 – 발음기호 – 품사 – 한글 뜻 – 영문 뜻〉 순서로 표기되어 있으며 빈도 표시(★)가 많을수록 필수 어휘입니다. 반복 등장하는 단어는 빈도 대신 '복습'으로 표기되어 있습니다. 품사는 아래와 같이 표기했습니다.

n. 명사 | a. 형용사 | ad. 부사 | v. 동사
conj. 접속사 | prep. 전치사 | int. 감탄사 | idiom 숙어 및 관용구

Comprehension Quiz

간단한 퀴즈를 통해 읽은 내용에 대한 이해력을 점검해 볼 수 있습니다.

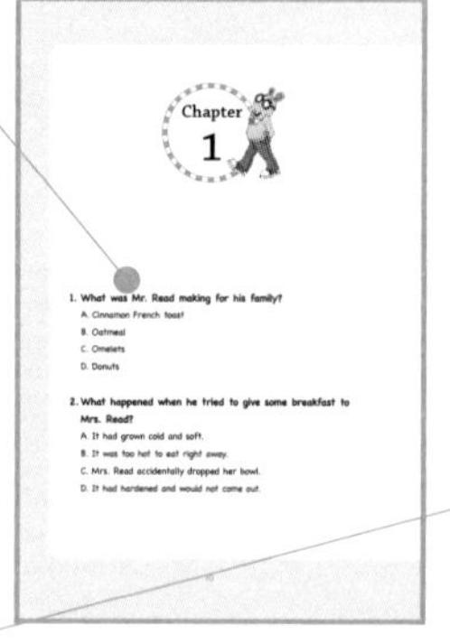
Chapter 1

1. What was Mr. Read making for his family?
A. Cinnamon French toast
B. Oatmeal
C. Omelets
D. Donuts

2. What happened when he tried to give some breakfast to Mrs. Read?
A. It had grown cold and soft.
B. It was too hot to eat right away.
C. Mrs. Read accidentally dropped her bowl.
D. It had hardened and would not come out.

번역

영문과 비교할 수 있도록 최대한 직역에 가까운 번역을 담았습니다.

오디오북 CD 구성

이 책은 '듣기 훈련'과 '소리 내어 읽기 훈련'을 위한 2가지 종류의 오디오북이 포함되어 있습니다.

- 듣기 훈련용 오디오북: 분당 145단어 속도 (미국 현지 판매 중인 오디오북)
- 소리 내어 읽기 훈련용 오디오북: 분당 110 단어 속도

오디오북은 MP3 파일로 제공되는 MP3 기기나 컴퓨터에 옮겨서 사용하셔야 합니다. 오디오북에 이상이 있을 경우 helper@longtailbooks.co.kr로 메일을 주시면 자세한 안내를 받으실 수 있습니다.

EBS 동영상 강의 안내

EBS의 어학사이트(EBSlang.co.kr)에서 『아서 챕터북』 동영상 강의가 진행되고 있습니다.
영어 어순의 원리에 맞게 빠르고 정확하게 이해하는 법을 완벽하게 코치해주는 국내 유일의 강의!
저렴한 수강료에 완강 시 50% 환급까지!
지금 바로 열광적인 수강 평가와 샘플 강의를 확인하세요!
http://Arthur.EnglishWish.com

1. What was Mr. Read making for his family?

A. Cinnamon French toast

B. Oatmeal

C. Omelets

D. Donuts

2. What happened when he tried to give some breakfast to Mrs. Read?

A. It had grown cold and soft.

B. It was too hot to eat right away.

C. Mrs. Read accidentally dropped her bowl.

D. It had hardened and would not come out.

3. How did Mr. Read feel about Crunch cereal?

A. He thought that it was too expensive.

B. He thought that it was a healthy choice for breakfast.

C. He thought that it would have you get cavities.

D. He thought that it used to taste better when he was younger.

4. Why was there a letter inside the Crunch cereal box?

A. It was an invitation to compete in the Crunch Cereal Jingle Contest.

B. It was an invitation to visit the Crunch cereal factory.

C. It was an order form to buy more Crunch cereal by mail.

D. It was a notice stating that Crunch cereal was coming out with a new flavor.

5. What did the small print in the letter read?

A. It read that the deadline was the next day.

B. It read that only children could compete in the contest.

C. It read that 20 boxtops were needed with each entry.

D. It read that the year's supply of Crunch cereal would all come at once.

Check Your Reading Speed

1분에 몇 단어를 읽는지 리딩 속도를 측정해보세요.

$$\frac{\text{485 words}}{\text{reading time (\qquad) sec}} \times 60 = (\qquad) \text{ WPM}$$

Build Your Vocabulary

touch [tʌʧ] n. 약간, 조금; 접촉, 만지기; v. 만지다, 닿다
A touch of something is a very small amount of it.

hint [hint] n. 미량, 조금; 힌트, 암시; v. 암시하다, 넌지시 말하다
A hint of something is a very small amount of it.

suspicion [səspíʃən] n. 아주 조금; 의심, 혐의, 용의
A suspicion of something is a very small amount of it.

stove [stouv] n. (요리용 가스·전기) 레인지; 스토브, 난로
A stove is a piece of equipment which provides heat, either for cooking or for heating a room.

latest [léitist] a. 최근의, 최신의
You use latest to describe something that is the most recent thing of its kind.

creation [kriéiʃən] n. 창작품; 창조, 창작
You can refer to something that someone has made as a creation, especially if it shows skill, imagination, or artistic ability.

steam [sti:m] n. 김, 안개; 증기, 수증기; v. 김을 내뿜다
Steam is the hot mist that forms when water boils.

pot [pat] n. 냄비, 솥
A pot is a deep round container used for cooking stews, soups, and other food.

swirl [swəːrl] v. 소용돌이치다, 빙빙 돌다; n. 소용돌이
If liquid or flowing swirls, it moves round and round quickly.

frost [frɔːst] v. 성에가 끼다; n. 서리, 성에 (forsted a. 서리에 뒤덮인)
Frosted glass is glass that you cannot see through clearly.

⋆ **chilly** [ʧíli] a. 차가운, 쌀쌀한; (태도 등이) 냉담한
If you feel chilly, you feel rather cold.

stick to one's ribs idiom (음식이) 영양가가 있다, 피가 되고 살이 되다
If some food stick to one's ribs, they last long and sustain people even in the coldest weather.

swivel [swívəl] v. 돌리다, 회전시키다; n. 회전 고리
If something swivels or if you swivel it, it turns around a central point so that it is facing in a different direction.

⋆⋆⋆ **present** [prizént] v. 내놓다, 건네주다; 증정하다, 바치다
If you present something, you bring, offer, or give it often in a formal or ceremonious way.

⋆⋆⋆ **please** [pliːz] v. 기쁘게 하다, 즐겁게 하다 (pleased a. 기뻐하는, 만족해 하는)
If you are pleased, you are happy about something or satisfied with something.

end up idiom 마침내는 (~으로) 되다[가다]; 끝나다
If you end up doing something or end up in a particular state, you do that thing or get into that state even though you did not originally intend to.

⋆ **recognition** [rèkəgníʃən] n. (공로 등에 대한) 인정, 표창; 알아봄, 인식
(in recognition of idiom ~을 인정하여, ~의 답례로)
If something is done in recognition of someone's achievements, it is done as a way of showing official appreciation of them.

⋆⋆ **support** [səpɔ́ːrt] n. 지지, 받침; v. 지지하다, 유지하다
If you give support to someone during a difficult or unhappy time, you are kind to them and help them.

★ **portion** [pɔ́:rʃən] n. (음식의) 1인분; 부분, 일부
A portion is the amount of food that is given to one person at a meal.

★ **tilt** [tilt] v. 기울이다, (뒤로) 젖히다; n. 기울어짐; 기울기
If you tilt an object or if it tilts, it moves into a sloping position with one end or side higher than the other.

★★ **spoon** [spu:n] v. 숟가락으로 떠서 옮기다; n. 숟가락, 스푼
If you spoon food into something, you put it there with an object which is shaped like a shallow bowl and has a long handle.

★★ **bowl** [boul] n. 그릇, 사발
A bowl is a round container with a wide uncovered top.

★ **harden** [ha:rdn] v. 굳다, 굳히다
When something hardens or when you harden it, it becomes stiff or firm.

★ **cement** [simént] n. 시멘트
Cement is a gray powder which is mixed with sand and water in order to make concrete.

★ **puzzle** [pʌzl] v. 곤혹스럽게 하다, 난처하게 하다; n. 수수께끼, 어려운 문제 (puzzled a. 어리둥절한)
If something puzzles you, you do not understand it and feel confused.

★ **react** [riækt] v. 화학 반응을 일으키다; 반응하다
When one chemical substance reacts with another, or when two chemical substances react, they combine chemically to form another substance.

★ **terrible** [térəbl] a. 끔찍한; 심한
A terrible experience or situation is very serious or very unpleasant.

★★★ **appear** [əpíər] v. ~인 듯하다, ~처럼 보이다; 나타나다, 생기다
If you say that something appears to be the way you describe it, you are reporting what you believe or what you have been told, though you cannot be sure it is true.

★★★ **mind** [maind] v. 신경 쓰다; 상관하다; 언짢아 하다
If you do not mind something, you are not annoyed or bothered by it.

close [klous] a. 아슬아슬한; 가까운
If you are close to something or if it is close, it is likely to happen or come soon.

whisper [hwíspəːr] v. 속삭이다; n. 속삭임
When you whisper, you say something very quietly.

nod [nad] v. (고개를) 끄덕이다, 끄덕여 나타내다; n. (고개를) 끄덕임, 까딱거림
If you nod, you move your head downwards and upwards to show agreement, understanding, or approval.

make do with idiom ~으로 임시 변통하다, 때우다
If you make do with something, you use or have it instead of something else that you do not have, although it is not as good.

cabinet [kǽbənit] n. 장식장, 캐비닛, 보관장
A cabinet is a cupboard used for storing things such as medicine or alcoholic drinks or for displaying decorative things in.

sink [siŋk] n. (부엌 등의) 싱크대, 개수대; v. 가라앉다, 빠지다; 침몰시키다
A sink is a large fixed container in a kitchen, with taps to supply water, which is mainly used for washing dishes.

bury [béri] v. 묻다, 파묻다, 매장하다
To bury something means to put it into a hole in the ground and cover it up with earth.

military [mílitèri] a. 군사의; 무력의; n. 군인들, 군대
Military means well-organized, controlled, or neat, in a way that is typical of a soldier.

honor [ánər] n. 경의, 존경; 명예
An honor is a special award that is given to someone, usually because they have done something good or because they are greatly respected.

favorite [féivərit] n. 좋아하는 물건, 마음에 드는 사람; a. 마음에 드는
If you refer to something or someone as your favorite, you mean that is or they are the one you like most.

★★ **appeal** [əpíːl] n. 매력; 호소, 애원; v. 매력적이다; 호소[간청]하다
The appeal of something is a quality that it has which people find attractive or interesting.

★ **coat** [kout] v. (막 같은 것을) 입히다; n. 외투, 코트 (sugar-coated a. 설탕옷을 입힌)
If you coat something with a substance or in a substance, you cover it with a thin layer of the substance.

★ **cardboard** [káːrdbɔ̀ːrd] n. 판지, 마분지
Cardboard is thick, stiff paper that is used, for example, to make boxes and models.

★ **stuff** [stʌf] n. 것(들), 물건, 물질; v. 채워 넣다, 채우다
You can use stuff to refer to things such as a substance, a collection of things, events, or ideas, or the contents of something in a general way without mentioning the thing itself by name.

★ **mouthful** [máuθfùl] n. (음식) 한 입, 한 모금
A mouthful of drink or food is the amount that you put or have in your mouth.

★ **cavity** [kǽvəti] n. 충치, (치아에 생긴) 구멍
In dentistry, a cavity is a hole in a tooth, caused by decay.

be willing to idiom 기꺼이 ~하는, 흔쾌히 ~하다
If someone is willing to do something, they are fairly happy about doing it.

★★ **risk** [risk] n. 위험; v. (~을) 위태롭게 하다
If there is a risk of something unpleasant, there is a possibility that it will happen.

serving [sə́ːrviŋ] n. (음식의) 1인분
A serving is an amount of food that is given to one person at a meal.

★ **envelope** [énvəlòup] n. 봉투
An envelope is the rectangular paper cover in which you send a letter to someone through the post.

note [nout] n. 편지, 쪽지; 메모, 필기; 음, 음표
A note is a short letter.

aloud [əláud] ad. 소리 내어, 큰 소리로
When you say something, read, or laugh aloud, you speak or laugh so that other people can hear you.

jingle [dʒiŋgl] n. (라디오 · 텔레비전의) 시엠송(광고방송용 노래); 딸랑, 짤랑
A jingle is a short, simple tune, often with words, which is used to advertise a product or program on radio or television.

contest [kántest] n. 대회, 시합; v. 경쟁을 벌이다, 다투다
A contest is a competition or game in which people try to win.

supply [səplái] n. 공급(량), 비축(량); v. 공급하다, 제공하다
A supply of something is an amount of it which someone has or which is available for them to use.

bet [bet] v. (~이) 틀림없다; (경마 · 내기 등에) 돈을 걸다; n. 내기; 내기 돈
You use expressions such as 'I bet', 'I'll bet', and 'you can bet' to indicate that you are sure something is true.

place [pleis] n. (경주 · 대회에서 입상권에 드는) 등위; 장소 (second place n. 2등)
Your place in a race or competition is your position in relation to the other competitors. If you are in first place, you are ahead of all the other competitors.

air [ɛər] v. 방송하다, 방송되다; n. 공기, 대기
If a broadcasting company airs a television or radio program, they show it on television or broadcast it on the radio.

commercial [kəmə́:rʃəl] n. (텔레비전 · 라디오의) 광고; a. 상업의, 무역의
A commercial is an advertisement that is broadcast on television or radio.

crunch [krʌntʃ] v. 아작아작[오도독] 씹다; n. 으드득 소리
If you crunch something hard, such as a sweet, you crush it noisily between your teeth.

☆**include** [inklúːd] v. ~을 포함하다, (~에) 포함시키다
If one thing includes another thing, it has the other thing as one of its parts.

☆**entry** [éntri] n. 응모권; 참가, 출입; 입장, 등장
An entry for a competition is a piece of work, for example a story or drawing, or the answers to a set of questions, which you complete in order to take part in the competition.

★**sigh** [sai] v. 한숨 쉬다; n. 한숨, 탄식
When you sigh, you let out a deep breath, as a way of expressing feelings such as disappointment, tiredness, or pleasure.

void [vɔid] a. 무효의, 법적 효력이 없는; n. (커다란) 빈 공간
Something that is void is officially considered to have no value or authority.

★**prohibit** [prouhíbit] v. (특히 법으로) 금하다; 금지하다
If a law or someone in authority prohibits something, they forbid it or make it illegal.

★**dump** [dʌmp] v. 쏟아 넣다; 버리다; v. 쓰레기 더미
If you dump something somewhere, you put it or unload it there quickly and carelessly.

1. **What did Arthur think of over the next few days?**

   A. Jingles

   B. Cereals

   C. Christmas

   D. Snowmen

2. **What did Arthur's mother suggest doing in order to clear his head?**

   A. She suggested that he watch TV for some inspiration.

   B. She suggested that he go play with D.W. outside.

   C. She suggested that he go for a walk with his friends.

   D. She suggested that he go outside to make a snowman.

3. How did D.W. feel about Arthur's snow sculpture?

A. She thought that it was too small.

B. She thought that it looked like a cat.

C. She thought that it looked like Crunch cereal.

D. She wanted to help Arthur build something together.

4. What job did Arthur give to D.W.?

A. D.W. was supposed to eat Crunch cereal.

B. D.W. was supposed to buy Crunch cereal.

C. D.W. was supposed to think of lyrics.

D. D.W. was supposed to ask her friends for ideas.

5. What did Arthur want to hit him?

A. A snowball

B. Inspiration

C. Lightning

D. Crunch cereal

Check Your Reading Speed
1분에 몇 단어를 읽는지 리딩 속도를 측정해보세요.

$$\frac{\text{476 words}}{\text{reading time (\quad\quad) sec}} \times 60 = (\quad\quad\quad) \text{ WPM}$$

Build Your Vocabulary

jingle [dʒiŋgl] n. (라디오·텔레비전의) 시엠송(광고방송용 노래); 딸랑, 짤랑
A jingle is a short, simple tune, often with words, which is used to advertise a product or program on radio or television.

⁑ **brush** [brʌʃ] v. 솔질을 하다; (솔이나 손으로) 털다
(brush one's teeth idiom 이를 닦다, 양치질을 하다)
If you brush your teeth, you clean your teeth with toothbrush and toothpaste.

crunch [krʌntʃ] n. 으드득 소리; v. 아작아작[오도독] 씹다
A crunch is a loud sound as something is pressed or crushed.

⁑ **bath** [bæθ] n. 목욕; 욕조; v. 목욕하다
When you have or take a bath, or when you are in the bath, you sit or lie in a bath filled with water in order to wash your body.

make up idiom (시 등을) 창작하다, (이야기 등을) 지어내다
If you make up a poem or a song, you write or compose it.

deadline [dédlain] n. 기한, 마감 시간[일자]
A deadline is a time or date before which a particular task must be finished or a particular thing must be done.

⁂ **break** [breik] n. (작업 중의) 휴식; 단절; 틈; v. 깨뜨리다, 부수다; 어기다
A break is a short period of time when you have a rest or a change from what you are doing.

recharge [riːʧáːrdʒ] v. 재충전하다 (recharge one's batteries idiom 휴식을 취하다)
If you recharge your batteries, you take a break from activities which are tiring or difficult in order to relax and feel better when you return to these activities.

* **creative** [kriéitiv] a. 창의적인, 창조적인, 독창적인
A creative person has the ability to invent and develop original ideas, especially in the arts.

** **clear** [kliər] v. 깨끗이 하다; 분명히 하다; a. 밝은, 맑은; 분명한, 뚜렷한
To clear your mind or your head means to free it from confused thoughts or from the effects of a drug such as alcohol.

** **roll** [roul] v. 굴리다, 굴러가다; n. 우르르[둥둥] 하는 소리
When something rolls or when you roll it, it moves along a surface, turning over many times.

** **chip** [ʧip] v. 쪼다, 깎다; n. 조각, 부스러기
If you chip something or if it chips, a small piece is broken off it.

* **sculpture** [skʌ́lpʧər] n. 조각, 조각상; v. 조각하다
A sculpture is a work of art that is produced by carving or shaping stone, wood, clay, or other materials.

*** **explain** [ikspléin] v. 설명하다, 분명하게 하다
If you explain something, you give details about it or describe it so that it can be understood.

rut [rʌt] n. 판[틀]에 박힌 생활; 바퀴 자국
If you say that someone is in a rut, you disapprove of the fact that they have become fixed in their way of thinking and doing things, and find it difficult to change.

** **insist** [insíst] v. 우기다, 주장하다
If you insist that something is the case, you say so very firmly and refuse to say otherwise, even though other people do not believe you.

be supposed to ~ idiom (관습·법·의무로) ~하기로 되어 있다
If you are supposed to do something, you are expected or required to do it according to a rule, a custom or an arrangement.

복습 **nod** [nad] v. (고개를) 끄덕이다, 끄덕여 나타내다; n. (고개를) 끄덕임, 까딱거림
If you nod, you move your head downward and upward to show agreement, understanding, or approval.

★★ **forget** [fərgét] v. 잊다, 깜빡하다
If you forget something or forget to do it, you fail to think about it or fail to remember to do it, for example because you are thinking about other things.

★★ **chest** [tʃest] ① n. 상자, 궤 ② n. 가슴, 흉부
A chest is a large, heavy box used for storing things.

★ **closet** [klázit] n. 벽장
A closet is a piece of furniture with doors at the front and shelves inside, which is used for storing things.

★★ **complain** [kəmpléin] v. 불평하다, 투덜거리다
If you complain about a situation, you say that you are not satisfied with it.

★★ **deal** [di:l] v. 취급하다, 다루다; 거래하다; 분배하다; n. 거래, 계약
If you deal with something, you solve its problem or carry out a task.

★ **impress** [imprés] v. 깊은 인상을 주다, 감명을 주다 (impressed a. 감명을 받은)
If something impresses you, you feel great admiration for it.

sort of idiom 어느 정도, 다소
You use sort of when you want to say that your description of something is not very accurate.

★ **rhyme** [raim] v. 운을 맞추다, 운을 맞춰 쓰다 n. 운(음조가 비슷한 글자);
If one word rhymes with another or if two words rhyme, they have a very similar sound.

★ **rhythm** [riðm] n. 리듬, 율동; 규칙적인 반복
A rhythm is a regular series of sounds or movements.

poetry [póuitri] n. 시, 시가
Poems, considered as a form of literature, are referred to as poetry.

attitude [ǽtitjù:d] n. 태도, 마음가짐; 자세
Your attitude to something is the way that you think and feel about it, especially when this shows in the way you behave.

flavor [fléivər] n. 풍미, 맛; v. 풍미를 더하다, 맛을 내다
The flavor of a food or drink is its taste.

combination [kàmbənéiʃən] n. 결합, 화합, 조합
A combination of things is a mixture of them.

melody [mélədi] n. 멜로디, 선율, 가락
A melody is a tune.

sigh [sai] v. 한숨 쉬다; n. 한숨, 탄식
When you sigh, you let out a deep breath, as a way of expressing feelings such as disappointment, tiredness, or pleasure.

inspiration [ìnspəréiʃən] n. 영감, 기발한 생각
Inspiration is a feeling of enthusiasm you get from someone or something, which gives you new and creative ideas.

flash [flæʃ] n. 번쩍임; 순간; v. (미소 등을 남에게) 얼른 보내다; 번쩍 비추다; 휙 지나가다
A flash is a sudden burst of light or of something shiny or bright.

lightning [láitniŋ] n. 번개, 번갯불
Lightning is the very bright flashes of light in the sky that happen during thunderstorms.

bull's-eye [bulz-ai] n. 명중, 적중; (과녁의) 중심, 정곡
The bull's-eye is the small circular area at the center of a target.

scoop [sku:p] v. 뜨다, 파다; 재빨리 들어 올리다; n. 국자, 주걱
If you scoop something from a container, you remove it with something such as a spoon.

1. What was Arthur doing during recess?

A. He was playing in the snow.

B. He was doing his homework inside.

C. He was in the school music room trying out note on the piano.

D. He was eating Crunch cereal with Buster to collect more boxtops.

2. What were the initial words of Arthur's jingle?

A. Buy Crunch

B. Eat Crunch

C. Try Crunch

D. Sweet Crunch

3. How did Buster suggest that Arthur think bigger?

A. He suggested posting a video online.

B. He suggested using a guitar instead of a piano.

C. He suggested getting more people and instruments.

D. He suggested making a story for the jingle.

4. Why was Francine so upset when Arthur met her?

A. She had needed help with her snow sculpture.

B. She had needed help with her homework.

C. Buster had broken her snow sculpture.

D. Nobody had taken a picture of her snow sculpture.

5. How did Francine react to Arthur's question about joining the band?

A. She said that she was too busy playing with the school band.

B. She said that she did not play any instruments.

C. She asked if Arthur had made a band before.

D. She asked when they started.

Check Your Reading Speed

1분에 몇 단어를 읽는지 리딩 속도를 측정해보세요.

$$\frac{490 \text{ words}}{\text{reading time (\qquad) sec}} \times 60 = (\qquad) \text{ WPM}$$

Build Your Vocabulary

empty [émpti] a. 비어 있는, 빈; v. 비우다
An empty place, vehicle, or container is one that has no people or things in it.

except [iksépt] prep. ~을 제외하고, ~이외에는
You use except for to introduce the only thing or person that prevents a statement from being completely true.

recess [risés] n. (학교의) 쉬는 시간; 휴식
A recess is a short period of time when you have a rest or a change from what you are doing.

note [nout] n. 음, 음표; 메모, 필기; 편지, 쪽지
In music, a note is the sound of a particular pitch, or a written symbol representing this sound.

silly [síli] a. 바보 같은, 어리석은; 유치한
If you say that someone or something is silly, you mean that they are foolish, childish, or ridiculous.

nod [nad] v. (고개를) 끄덕이다, 끄덕여 표시하다; n. (고개를) 끄덕임, 까딱거림
If you nod, you move your head downward and upward to show agreement, understanding, or approval.

bang [bæŋ] v. 쾅 닫다, 탕 치다, 부딪치다; n. 쾅하는 소리
If you bang a door or if it bangs, it closes suddenly with a loud noise.

복습 **jingle** [dʒiŋgl] n. (라디오·텔레비전의) 시엠송(광고방송용 노래); 딸랑, 짤랑
A jingle is a short, simple tune, often with words, which is used to advertise a product or program on radio ortelevision.

★★ **melt** [melt] v. 녹다, 녹이다; (감정 등이) 누그러지다
When a solid substance melts or when you melt it, it changes to a liquid, usually because it has been heated.

★ **drip** [drip] v. 방울방울[뚝뚝] 떨어지다; n. 방울져 떨어지는 것, (물)방울
When something drips, drops of liquid fall from it.

★★ **throat** [θrout] n. 목구멍; 목 (clear one's throat idiom 목을 가다듬다, 헛기침하다)
Your throat is the back of your mouth and the top part of the tubes that go down into your stomach and your lungs.

think something over idiom ~을 심사숙고하다
If you think something over, you consider something carefully, especially before making a decision.

make sense idiom 뜻이 통하다, 도리에 맞다
If something makes sense, it has a meaning that you can easily understand.

★ **tune** [tju:n] n. 곡조, 선율; v. 조율하다, 조정하다
A tune is a series of musical notes that is pleasant and easy to remember.

★★ **instrument** [ínstrəmənt] n. 악기; 기구, 도구
A musical instrument is an object such as a piano, guitar, or flute, which you play in order to produce music.

★★ **musician** [mju:zíʃən] n. 음악가(연주자·작곡가), 뮤지션
A musician is a person who plays a musical instrument as their job or hobby.

come up with idiom ~을 생각해 내다, ~을 내놓다
If you come up with a plan or idea, you think of it and suggest it.

audition [ɔːdíʃən] n. 오디션; v. 오디션을 보다
An audition is a short performance given by an actor, dancer, or musician so that a director or conductor can decide if they are good enough to be in a play, film, or orchestra.

and everything idiom 등등, 이것저것 다
And everything means and so on, or and other similar things.

* **check** [ʧek] v. 조사하다, 점검하다, 확인하다
If you check on someone or something, you make sure they are in a safe or satisfactory condition.

복습 **bet** [bet] v. (~이) 틀림없다; (경마·내기 등에) 돈을 걸다; n. 내기; 내기 돈
You use expressions such as 'I bet', 'I'll bet', and 'you can bet' to indicate that you are sure something is true.

* **grab** [græb] v. 움켜쥐다, 부여잡다; n. 부여잡기
If you grab something, you take it or pick it up suddenly and roughly.

* **yard** [jaːrd] n. (학교의) 운동장; 마당, 뜰
A yard is a piece of land next to someone's house, with grass and plants growing in it.

bundle up idiom ~를 따뜻이 둘러싸다
If you bundle someone up, you make them feel warmer by putting warm clothes on them or covering them with blankets.

* **pile** [pail] n. 쌓아 놓은 것, 더미; v. 쌓다, 포개다
If you talk about a pile of something or piles of something, you mean a large amount of it.

복습 **sigh** [sai] v. 한숨 쉬다; n. 한숨, 탄식
When you sigh, you let out a deep breath, as a way of expressing feelings such as disappointment, tiredness, or pleasure.

복습 **sculpture** [skʌ́lpʧər] n. 조각, 조각상; v. 조각하다
A sculpture is a work of art that is produced by carving or shaping stone, wood, clay, or other materials.

end [end] v. (질·정도에서) 능가하다, 웃돌다; 끝나다, 마치다
If you describe something as, for example, the deal to end all deals or the film to end all films, you mean that it is very important or successful, and that compared to it all other deals or films seem second-rate.

bold [bould] a. 용감한, 대담한; 선명한, 굵은
Someone who is bold is not afraid to do things which involve risk or danger.

daring [déəriŋ] a. 대담한; 위험한; n. 대담성
A daring person is willing to do things that might be dangerous.

wonder [wʌ́ndəːr] v. 호기심을 가지다, 이상하게 여기다; n. 경탄할 만한 것, 경이
If you wonder about something, you think about it because it interests you and you want to know more about it.

dumb [dʌm] a. 멍청한, 바보 같은; 벙어리의, 말을 못 하는
If you say that something is dumb, you think that it is silly and annoying.

forgive [fərgív] v. 용서하다; (빚·의무 등을) 면제하다
If you forgive someone who has done something bad or wrong, you stop being angry with them and no longer want to punish them.

pain [pein] n. 고통, 아픔; v. 아프게 하다, 고통을 주다
If you are in pain, you feel pain in a part of your body, because you are injured or ill.

widen [waidn] v. 커지다; 넓어지다; 넓히다
If you widen something or if it widens, it becomes greater in measurement from one side or edge to the other.

kick [kik] n. 차기, 발길질; v. (발로) 차다
If you give a kick at someone or something, you hit them forcefully with your foot.

1. What happened in Arthur's dream?

A. He was eating Crunch cereal.

B. He was being booed in a concert hall.

C. He was playing well with a full band.

D. His band had gotten sick from too much Crunch cereal.

2. What were the children doing at Arthur's house?

A. They were there to help Arthur clean his garage.

B. They were there to eat Arthur's father latest dessert.

C. They were there to let Arthur borrow their instruments.

D. They were there to audition for Arthur's band.

3. How did Arthur feed everyone?

A. He had put out bowls of Crunch cereal.

B. He had offered to take them to the Sugar Bowl.

C. He had asked his father to make oatmeal for everyone.

D. He had asked his parents to order pizza.

4. What did Grandma Thora play?

A. Saxophone

B. Piano

C. Harp

D. Harmonica

5. What was the condition for Binky to join the band?

A. He had to be nicer to Arthur.

B. He had to pay to join the band.

C. He had to finish the last box of Crunch cereal.

D. He had to help Arthur think of words to his jingle.

Check Your Reading Speed
1분에 몇 단어를 읽는지 리딩 속도를 측정해보세요.

$$\frac{545 \text{ words}}{\text{reading time (} \quad \text{) sec}} \times 60 = (\quad) \text{ WPM}$$

Build Your Vocabulary

** **hall** [hɔ:l] n. 넓은 방[건물]; (건물 입구 안쪽의) 현관; (건물의) 복도, 통로
(concert hall n. 콘서트홀, 연주회장)
A hall is a large room or building which is used for public events such as concerts, exhibitions, and meetings.

* **stare** [stɛər] v. 응시하다, 뚫어지게 보다
If you stare at someone or something, you look at them for a long time.

** **audience** [ɔ́:diəns] n. 청중, 관객
The audience at a play, concert, film, or public meeting is the group of people watching or listening to it.

* **critic** [krítik] n. 비평가, 평론가
A critic is a person who writes about and expresses opinions about things such as books, films, music, or art.

복습 **jingle** [dʒiŋgl] n. (라디오·텔레비전의) 시엠송(광고방송용 노래); 딸랑, 짤랑
A jingle is a short, simple tune, often with words, which is used to advertise a product or program on radio or television.

** **microphone** [máikrəfòun] n. 마이크(로폰)
A microphone is a device that is used to make sounds louder or to record them on a tape recorder.

announce [ənáuns] v. 알리다, 공고하다, 전하다
If you announce a piece of news or an intention, especially something that people may not like, you say it loudly and clearly, so that everyone you are with can hear it.

boo [bu:] v. (우우 하고) 야유하다; n. 야유 (소리)
If you boo a speaker or performer, you shout 'boo' or make other loud sounds to indicate that you do not like them.

fly [flai] v. (flew-flown) (비행기를) 타다[타고 가다]; 날다, 비행하다
If you fly somewhere, you travel there in an aircraft.

instrument [ínstrəmənt] n. 악기; 기구, 도구
A musical instrument is an object such as a piano, guitar, or flute, which you play in order to produce music.

patch [pætʃ] v. 때우다, 덧대다 ; n. 조각, 부분
If you patch something that has a hole in it, you mend it by fastening a patch over the hole.

waste [weist] v. (돈·시간 등을) 낭비하다, 허비하다; n. 낭비
If you waste something such as time, money, or energy, you use too much of it doing something that is not important or necessary, or is unlikely to succeed.

explain [ikspléin] v. 설명하다, 분명하게 하다
If you explain something, you give details about it or describe it so that it can be understood.

snap out of it idiom (침울해 하지 말고) 기운을 내다
If you say 'snap out of it' to someone, you mean they should try to stop feeling unhappy or depressed.

blink [bliŋk] v. 눈을 깜박이다; n. 눈을 깜빡거림
When you blink or when you blink your eyes, you shut your eyes and very quickly open them again.

* **snap** [snæp] v. 홱 움직이다; 손가락을 튕기다; 딱[툭] (하고) 부러뜨리다; n. 딱[탁] 하는 소리
If you snap something into a particular position, or if it snaps into that position, it moves quickly into that position, with a sharp sound.

** **ignore** [ignɔ́:r] v. 무시하다, 모르는 체하다
If you ignore someone or something, you pay no attention to them.

*** **sign** [sain] n. 표지판, 표시; 징후, 흔적; v. 서명하다; 신호를 보내다
A sign is a piece of wood, metal, or plastic with words or pictures on it. Signs give you information about something, or give you a warning or an instruction.

복습 **audition** [ɔ:díʃən] v. 오디션을 보다; n. 오디션
If you audition or if someone auditions you, you do a short performance so that a director or conductor can decide if you are good enough to be in a play, film, or orchestra.

* **garage** [gərá:dʒ] n. 차고, 주차장
A garage is a building in which you keep a car. A garage is often built next to or as part of a house.

*** **form** [fɔ:rm] v. 형성되다, 구성하다, 만들어내다; n. 모양, 형태; 서식
When a particular shape forms or is formed, people or things move or are arranged so that this shape is made.

take charge of idiom ~의 책임을 지다
If you take charge of someone or something, you make yourself responsible for them and take control over them.

relieved [rilí:vd] a. 안도하는, 다행으로 여기는
If you are relieved, you feel happy because something unpleasant has not happened or is no longer happening.

*** **business** [bíznis] n. 사업, 일; 사건
Business is work or some other activity that you do as part of your job and not for pleasure.

☆ **ambitious** [æmbíʃəs] a. 야심 있는
An ambitious idea or plan is on a large scale and needs a lot of work to be carried out successfully.

☆ **pause** [pɔːz] v. (말·일을 하다가) 잠시 멈추다; n. (말·행동 등의) 멈춤
If you pause while you are doing something, you stop for a short period and then continue.

☆ **expect** [ikspékt] v. 예상[기대]하다; 요구하다
If you expect something, or expect a person to do something, you believe that it is your right to have that thing, or the person's duty to do it for you.

☆ **feed** [fiːd] v. 먹이다; 먹을 것을 먹다
To feed a family or a community means to supply food for them.

복습 **bowl** [boul] n. 그릇, 사발
A bowl is a round container with a wide uncovered top.

eat up idiom (~을) 다 먹다
If you eat up, you eat all the food you have been given.

☆ **plenty** [plénti] n. 많음, 가득, 풍부한 양
If there is plenty of something, there is a large amount of it.

복습 **crunch** [krʌntʃ] v. 아작아작[오도독] 씹다; n. 으드득 소리
If you crunch something hard, such as a sweet, you crush it noisily between your teeth.

riff [rif] n. 리프, 반복 악절
In jazz and rock music, a riff is a short repeated tune.

복습 **note** [nout] n. 음, 음표; 메모, 필기; 편지, 쪽지
In music, a note is the sound of a particular pitch, or a written symbol representing this sound.

★ **rattle** [rætl] v. 달가닥거리다, 덜컹거리다; n. 덜거덕거리는 소리
When something rattles or when you rattle it, it makes short sharp knocking sounds because it is being shaken or it keeps hitting against something hard.

★ **horn** [hɔːrn] n. 피리; (차량의) 경적; (양·소 등의) 뿔
A horn is a musical instrument of the brass family, which is a long circular metal tube, wide at one end.

★ **faint** [feint] v. 기절하다; n. 기절, 졸도; a. 희미한, 어렴풋한
If you faint, you lose consciousness for a short time, especially because you are hungry, or because of pain, heat, or shock.

tryout [tráiaut] n. 시험해 보기, 테스트하기
If you give something a tryout, you try it or test it to see how useful it is.

★★ **treatment** [tríːtmənt] n. 대우, 취급; 치료, 처치
Your treatment of someone is the way you behave toward them or deal with them.

never mind idiom (중요하지 않으니까) 신경 쓰지 마, 괜찮아
You use never mind to tell someone that they do not need to do something or worry about something, because it is not important or because you will do it yourself.

listen up idiom 잘 듣다, 진지하게 듣다
If you say someone to listen up, you tell them to pay attention to what you are going to say.

jazzy [dʒǽzi] a. 재즈 같은
Something that is jazzy resembles with jazz music.

★★★ **draw** [drɔː] v. (drew-drawn) 끌다, 당기다; 그리다; n. 추첨; 무승부
If you draw someone's attention to something, you make them aware of it or make them think about it.

★★ **attention** [əténʃən] n. 주의, 관심; 배려
If you give someone or something your attention, you look at it, listen to it, or think about it carefully.

brand-new [brǽnd-njúː] a. 신상품의, 아주 새로운
A brand-new object is completely new.

⋆ **groove** [gruːv] v. 리듬을 타다; n. (음악의) 리듬
If you groove, you join by an enjoyable rhythm.

복습 **impress** [imprés] v. 깊은 인상을 주다, 감명을 주다 (impressed a. 감명을 받은)
If something impresses you, you feel great admiration for it.

⋆ **hire** [haiər] v. 고용하다, 쓰다; 빌리다; n. 신입사원; 대여
If you hire someone, you employ them or pay them to do a particular job for you.

복습 **nod** [nad] v. (고개를) 끄덕이다, 끄덕여 나타내다; n. (고개를) 끄덕임, 까딱거림
If you nod, you move your head downward and upward to show agreement, understanding, or approval.

⋆⋆ **complicated** [kámpləkèitid] a. 복잡한, 이해하기 어려운
If you say that something is complicated, you mean it has so many parts or aspects that it is difficult to understand or deal with.

⋆ **stalk** [stɔːk] ① v. 활보하다, 으스대며 걷다; 몰래 접근하다 ② n. 줄기, 잎자루
If you stalk somewhere, you walk there in a stiff, proud, or angry way.

⋆ **absolute** [ǽbsəluːt] a. 완전한, 무조건의, 절대적인 (absolutely ad. 절대적으로, 무조건)
Absolute means total and complete.

⋆⋆⋆ **condition** [kəndíʃən] n. 조건; 상태, 상황
When you agree to do something on condition that something else happens, you mean that you will only do it if this other thing also happens.

복습 **deal** [diːl] n. 거래, 계약; v. 거래하다; 취급하다, 다루다; 분배하다
If you make a deal, do a deal, or cut a deal, you complete an agreement or an arrangement with someone, especially in business.

1. What was the name of Arthur's band?

A. Crunch Bunch

B. Crunch Munch

C. Crunch Band

D. Crunch Stars

2. What role did D.W. want in Arthur's band?

A. She wanted to sing.

B. She wanted to be in charge.

C. She wanted to play an instrument.

D. She wanted to feed the band members.

3. How did Arthur feel about the others suggestions?

A. He liked everyone's suggestions.

B. He wanted them to play it his way.

C. He wanted everyone to speak individually.

D. He wanted everyone to go home.

4. What did the band play from?

A. Arthur humming

B. A tape recording

C. Sheet music

D. The school's music teacher

5. Which of the following was not one of the reactions to the sound?

A. The barber was startled and clipped off Miss Tingley's bangs.

B. Snow fell from some branches on Mrs. Tibble.

C. Muffy's parents thought it was an air raid.

D. The garage windows shattered.

Check Your Reading Speed

1분에 몇 단어를 읽는지 리딩 속도를 측정해보세요.

$$\frac{515 \text{ words}}{\text{reading time (\quad) sec}} \times 60 = (\quad) \text{ WPM}$$

Build Your Vocabulary

복습 **form** [fɔ:rm] v. 구성하다, 형성되다, 만들어내다; n. 모양, 형태; 서식
If you form an organization, group, or company, you start it.

★ **bunch** [bʌntʃ] n. 떼, 한패; 다발, 송이; 다량
A bunch of people is a group of people who share one or more characteristics or who are doing something together.

복습 **include** [inklú:d] v. ~을 포함하다, (~에) 포함시키다
If one thing includes another thing, it has the other thing as one of its parts.

복습 **instrument** [ínstrəmənt] n. 악기; 기구, 도구
A musical instrument is an object such as a piano, guitar, or flute, which you play in order to produce music.

in charge idiom ~을 맡고 있는, 담당의
If you have charge of or are in charge of something or someone, you have responsibility for them.

★★★ **firm** [fə:rm] ① a. 단호한, 확고한; 단단한; 견고한 (firmly ad. 단호히) ② n. 회사
If you describe someone as firm, you mean they behave in a way that shows that they are not going to change their mind, or that they are the person who is in control.

★ **invisible** [invízəbl] a. 보이지 않는, 볼 수 없는
If you describe something as invisible, you mean that it cannot be seen, for example because it is transparent, hidden, or very small.

stuck [stʌk] a. 꽉 끼인, 갇힌, 움직일 수 없는; v. STICK의 과거·과거분사
If something is stuck in a particular position, it is fixed tightly in this position and is unable to move.

snowbank [snóubæŋk] n. (산허리·계곡의) 눈 더미
A snowbank is a mound or slope of snow.

복습 **check** [ʧek] v. 조사하다, 점검하다, 확인하다
If you check on someone or something, you make sure they are in a safe or satisfactory condition.

★ **mutter** [mʌ́tər] v. 중얼거리다, 불평하다; n. 중얼거림, 불평
If you mutter, you speak very quietly so that you cannot easily be heard, often because you are complaining about something.

bossy [bási] a. 우두머리 행세를 하는, 다른 사람을 쥐고 흔드는
If you describe someone as bossy, you mean that they enjoy telling people what to do.

start off idiom (~하는 것으로) 시작하다
If you start off, you begin doing something in a particular way.

복습 **bang** [bæŋ] n. 쾅 하는 소리; v. 탕 치다, 부딪치다, 쾅 닫다
A bang is a sudden loud noise such as the noise of an explosion.

복습 **note** [nout] n. 음, 음표; 메모, 필기; 편지, 쪽지
In music, a note is the sound of a particular pitch, or a written symbol representing this sound.

복습 **stare** [stɛər] v. 응시하다, 뚫어지게 보다
If you stare at someone or something, you look at them for a long time.

★★★ **raise** [reiz] v. 들어올리다, 들다; 키우다, 기르다
If you raise something, you move it so that it is in a higher position.

roll one's eyes idiom 눈을 굴리다
If you roll your eyes, you show with your eyes that you don't believe someone or aren't interested in what they're saying.

복습 **roll** [roul] n. 우르르[둥둥] 하는 소리; v. 굴리다, 굴러가다
A roll of drums is a long, low, fairly loud sound made by drums.

⋆ **dramatic** [drəmǽtik] a. 극적인; 인상적인, 감격적인
A dramatic change or event happens suddenly and is very noticeable and surprising.

⋆ **impact** [ímpækt] n. 효과; 충격, 충돌
The impact that something has on a situation, process, or person is a sudden and powerful effect that it has on them.

⋆⋆ **chin** [tʃin] n. 턱
Your chin is the part of your face that is below your mouth and above your neck.

⋆⋆ **string** [striŋ] n. (오케스트라의) 현악기부, 현악기 연주자들; 끈, 실; v. 묶다, 매달다
The strings are the section of an orchestra which consists of stringed instruments played with a bow.

⋆ **pluck** [plʌk] v. (악기의 현을) 튀기다, 켜다; 잡아뜯다, 뜯어내다
If you pluck a guitar or other musical instrument, you pull the strings with your fingers and let them go, so that they make a sound.

복습 **horn** [hɔːrn] n. 피리; (차량의) 경적; (양·소 등의) 뿔
A horn is a musical instrument of the brass family, which is a long circular metal tube, wide at one end.

⋆⋆ **wave** [weiv] v. 흔들다, 신호하다; 파도치다; n. 파도, 물결
If you wave or wave your hand, you move your hand from side to side in the air, usually in order to say hello or goodbye to someone.

⋆⋆ **silence** [sáiləns] n. 고요, 적막, 정적; 침묵
The silence of a place is the extreme quietness there.

deafen [défən] v. 귀를 먹먹하게 하다 (deafening a. 귀청이 터질 것 같은)
If a noise deafens you, it is so loud that you cannot hear anything else at the same time.

복습 **entry** [éntri] n. 응모권; 참가, 출입; 입장, 등장 (entry form n. 참가 신청서)
An entry for a competition is a piece of work, for example a story or drawing, or the answers to a set of questions, which you complete in order to take part in the competition.

복습 **jingle** [dʒiŋgl] n. (라디오 · 텔레비전의) 시엠송(광고방송용 노래); 딸랑, 짤랑
A jingle is a short, simple tune, often with words, which is used to advertise a product or program on radio or television.

carry on idiom ~을 계속하다
If you carry on, you continue doing something or moving in a particular direction, without stopping.

★★★ **pass** [pæs] v. 건네주다; 지나가다, 통과하다; n. 통행, 통과
If you pass something to someone, you take it in your hand and give it to them.

sheet music [ʃiːt mjúːzik] n. 한 곡 단위로 인쇄한 악보
Sheet music is music that is printed on sheets of paper without a hard cover.

★★ **repeat** [ripíːt] v. 반복하다, 되풀이하다
If you repeat an action, you do it again.

★ **motion** [móuʃən] v. 몸짓으로 알리다; n. 운동, 동작
If you motion to someone, you move your hand or head as a way of telling them to do something or telling them where to go.

★★★ **strange** [streindʒ] a. 이상한, 낯선
Something that is strange is unusual or unexpected, and makes you feel slightly nervous or afraid.

복습 **garage** [gərάːdʒ] n. 차고, 주차장
A garage is a building in which you keep a car. A garage is often built next to or as part of a house.

★★★ **direction** [dirékʃən] n. 방향; 지도, 지시
A direction is the general line that someone or something is moving or pointing in.

sidewalk [sáidwɔ̀:k] n. (포장한) 보도, 인도
A sidewalk is a path with a hard surface by the side of a road.

branch [bræntʃ] n. 나뭇가지; 지사, 분점
The branches of a tree are the parts that grow out from its trunk and have leaves, flowers, or fruit growing on them.

overhead [óuvərhed] ad. 머리 위에, 높이; a. 머리 위의, 상공의
You use overhead to indicate that something is above you or above the place that you are talking about.

powder [páudər] v. 가루로 만들다, 제분하다; n. 가루, 분말
(powdered sugar n. 분말 설탕)
A powdered substance is one which is in the form of a powder although it can come in a different form.

barber [bá:rbər] n. 이발사
A barber is a man whose job is cutting men's hair.

blast [blæst] v. 크게 울리다; 폭발시키다; n. 빵[삑] 하는 소리; 폭발
If you blast something such as a car horn, or if it blasts, it makes a sudden, loud sound.

startle [sta:rtl] v. 깜짝 놀라게 하다; 움찔하다; n. 깜짝 놀람 (startled a. 놀란)
If something sudden and unexpected startles you, it surprises and frightens you slightly.

clip [klip] v. 자르다, 깎다; 클립으로 고정시키다; 쥐다; n. 깎음; 클립
If you clip something, you cut small pieces from it, especially in order to shape it.

weaken [wí:kən] v. 약해지다, 힘이 빠지다
If you weaken something or if it weakens, it becomes less strong or less powerful.

edge [edʒ] n. 끝, 가장자리, 모서리
The edge of something is the place or line where it stops, or the part of it that is furthest from the middle.

pack a punch idiom 강렬한 효과를 가지다, 펀치력이 있다
If something packs a punch, it has a powerful effect on someone.

* **raid** [reid] n. 습격, 급습; v. 습격하다
When soldiers raid a place, they make a sudden armed attack against it, with the aim of causing damage rather than occupying any of the enemy's land.

** **remind** [rimáind] v. 생각나게 하다, 상기시키다, 일깨우다
If someone reminds you of a fact or event that you already know about, they say something which makes you think about it.

take chances idiom 운에 맡기다, (모험치고) 해보다
When you take chances, you try to do something although there is a large risk of danger or failure.

*** **spend** [spend] v. (시간을) 보내다, 지내다; (돈·자원을) 쓰다, 소비하다
If you spend time or energy doing something, you use your time or effort doing it.

* **shelter** [ʃéltər] n. 대피처, 피신처; 주거지; v. 쉴 곳을 제공하다, 보호하다
(bomb shelter n. 공습 대피소, 방공호)
A shelter is a small building or covered place which is made to protect people from bad weather or danger.

may as well idiom ~하는 편이 좋다
If you may as well do something, you will do it because it seems best in the situation that you are in, although you may not really want to do it.

** **basement** [béismənt] n. (건물의) 지하층
The basement of a building is a floor built partly or completely below ground level.

1. Why did the police officer come to Arthur's garage?

A. She had heard that a dog was being tortured.

B. She had heard that many children were missing.

C. She had heard complaints about the noise.

D. She had seen Arthur's garage windows break.

2. What advice did the police officer give Arthur?

A. She told Arthur to practice in a music room.

B. She told Arthur to get out of his garage.

C. She told Arthur to keep the volume down.

D. She told Arthur to use less instruments.

3. Why did the other band members leave after the police officer came?

A. They were too afraid to play again.

B. They wanted to take a break for lunch.

C. They wanted to quit the band permanently.

D. They wanted to call their parents.

4. How did Buster tell Arthur he felt after eating lunch?

A. He told Arthur that he always thought better on a full stomach.

B. He told Arthur that he always felt more relaxed after eating.

C. He told Arthur that he always thought about food.

D. He told Arthur that he always rewarded himself by eating.

5. Why did Arthur not want to take a break?

A. He said that he had a lot of stress.

B. He said that he was hungry.

C. He said that he was not tired.

D. He said that he was dedicated.

Check Your Reading Speed

1분에 몇 단어를 읽는지 리딩 속도를 측정해보세요.

$$\frac{473 \text{ words}}{\text{reading time (} \quad \text{) sec}} \times 60 = (\quad) \text{ WPM}$$

Build Your Vocabulary

복습 **garage** [gərá:dʒ] n. 차고, 주차장

A garage is a building in which you keep a car. A garage is often built next to or as part of a house.

복습 **stare** [stɛər] v. 응시하다, 뚫어지게 보다

If you stare at someone or something, you look at them for a long time.

복습 **bang** [bæŋ] n. 쾅 하는 소리; v. 탕 치다, 부딪치다, 쾅 닫다

A bang is a sudden loud noise such as the noise of an explosion.

** **knock** [nak] n. 노크, 문 두드리는 소리; v. 부딪치다, 충돌하다; (문을) 두드리다, 노크하다

A knock is a sudden short noise made when someone or something hits a door.

* **officer** [ɔ́:fisər] n. 경찰관; 장교 (police officer n. 경찰관)

Members of the police force can be referred to as officers.

cruiser [krú:zər] n. 순찰차; 순항보트

A cruiser is a police car.

복습 **flash** [flæʃ] v. 번쩍 비추다; 휙 지나가다, (미소 등을 남에게) 얼른 보내다; n. 번쩍임; 순간

If a light flashes or if you flash a light, it shines with a sudden bright light, especially as quick, regular flashes of light.

* **investigate** [invéstəgèit] v. 수사하다, 조사하다, 살피다; 연구하다

If someone, especially an official, investigates an event, situation, or claim, they try to find out what happened or what is the truth.

★ **complaint** [kəmpléint] n. 불평, 항의
A complaint is a statement in which you express your dissatisfaction with a particular situation.

복습 **note** [nout] n. 메모, 필기; 편지, 쪽지; 음, 음표
A note is something that you write down to remind yourself of something.

★ **torture** [tɔ́:rʧər] v. 고문하다; 지독히 괴롭히다
If someone is tortured, another person deliberately causes them great pain over a period of time, in order to punish them or to make them reveal information.

take a dim view of idiom ~을 비관적으로 보다
If you take a dim view or a poor view of someone or something, you disapprove of them or have a low opinion of them.

★★★ **honest** [ánist] ad. 정말로, 참으로; a. 정직한, 솔직한
You say 'honest' before or after a statement to emphasize that you are telling the truth and that you want people to believe you.

siren [sáirən] n. 사이렌, 경적
A siren is a warning device which makes a long, loud noise.

unauthorized [ʌnɔ́:θəràizd] a. 공인되지 않은
If something is unauthorized, it has been produced or is happening without official permission.

★★ **fancy** [fǽnsi] a. 화려한, 고급스러운; v. 원하다, ~하고 싶다; n. 공상, 상상
If you describe something as fancy, you mean that it is special, unusual, or elaborate, for example because it has a lot of decoration.

rehearse [rihə́:rs] v. 예행연습을 하다, 리허설을 하다
When people rehearse a play, dance, or piece of music, they practice it in order to prepare for a performance.

복습 **jingle** [dʒiŋgl] n. (라디오·텔레비전의) 시엠송(광고방송용 노래); 딸랑, 짤랑
A jingle is a short, simple tune, often with words, which is used to advertise a product or program on radio or television.

* **scan** [skæn] v. 훑어보다, 살피다; 자세히 조사하다; 스캔하다; n. 정밀 검사; 스캔
When you scan a place or group of people, you look at it carefully, usually because you are looking for something or someone.

* **pad** [pæd] n. 필기첩, 메모지의 묶음
A pad of paper is a number of pieces of paper which are fixed together along the top or the side, so that each piece can be torn off when it has been used.

in order idiom 적법한; 제대로 된
If something is in order, it is all correct and legal.

jangle [dʒǽŋgl] v. 쨍그렁 거리다; 신경을 거슬리게 하다
When objects strike against each other and make an unpleasant ringing noise, you can say that they jangle or are jangled.

복습 **nod** [nad] v. (고개를) 끄덕이다, 끄덕여 나타내다; n. (고개를) 끄덕임, 까딱거림
If you nod, you move your head downward and upward to show agreement, understanding, or approval.

복습 **close** [klous] a. 아슬아슬한; 가까운
If you are close to something or if it is close, it is likely to happen or comesoon. If you are close to doing something, you are likely to do it soon.

make the newspaper idiom 신문에 나다
If you make the newspaper, you become newsworthy and are printed in the newspaper.

* **pack** [pæk] v. (짐을) 싸다, 꾸리다; 가지다, 지니다
When you pack a bag, you put clothes and other things into it, because you are leaving a place or going on holiday.

복습 **tune** [tjuːn] n. 곡조, 선율; v. 조율하다, 조정하다
A tune is a series of musical notes that is pleasant and easy to remember.

give up idiom 포기하다, 단념하다
If you give up, you decide that you cannot do something and stop trying to do it.

arrest [ərést] v. 체포하다, 저지하다; (주의·이목·흥미 등을) 끌다; n. 체포, 검거, 구속
If the police arrest you, they take charge of you and take you to a police station, because they believe you may have committed a crime.

build [bild] v. 만들어 내다; 짓다, 건축하다
If you build something, you make it by joining things together.

jail [dʒeil] n. 교도소, 감옥; v. 수감하다
A jail is a place where criminals are kept in order to punish them, or where people waiting to be tried are kept.

calendar [kǽləndər] n. 일정표, 달력
A calendar is a chart or device which displays the date and the day of the week, and often the whole of a particular year divided up into months, weeks, and days.

복습 **contest** [kántest] n. 대회, 시합; v. 경쟁을 벌이다, 다투다
A contest is a competition or game in which people try to win.

sidestep [sáidstèp] v. (몸을 옆으로 움직여) 피하다; (대답·문제 처리를) 회피하다
If you sidestep, you step sideways in order to avoid something or someone that is coming toward you or going to hit you.

inspire [inspáiər] v. 영감을 주다; 고무하다, 격려하다; (감정 등을) 불어넣다
(inspired a. 영감을 받은)
If someone or something inspires you, they give you new ideas and a strong feeling of enthusiasm.

discourage [diskə́:ridʒ] v. 낙담시키다, 실망시키다 (discouraged a. 낙심한)
If someone or something discourages you, they cause you to lose your enthusiasm about your actions.

file [fail] v. 줄지어 가다; (문서 등을 정리하여) 보관하다, 철하다; n. 줄, 파일
When a group of people files somewhere, they walk one behind the other in a line.

knot [nat] n. (긴장·화 등으로 복부·목 등이) 뻣뻣한 느낌; 매듭; v. 매듭을 묶다
If you feel a knot in your stomach, you get an uncomfortable tight feeling in your stomach, usually because you are afraid or excited.

spin [spin] v. (spun-spun) (빙빙) 돌다, 회전하다
If something spins or if you spin it, it turns quickly around a central point.

break [breik] n. (작업 중의) 휴식; 단절; 틈; v. 깨뜨리다, 부수다; 어기다
A break is a short period of time when you have a rest or a change from what you are doing.

spell [spel] v. (단어의) 철자를 쓰다[말하다], 철자를 맞게 쓰다
When you spell a word, you write or speak each letter in the word in the correct order.

much less idiom 하물며[더구나] ~은 아니다
You use the expressions still less, much less, and even less after a negative statement in order to introduce and emphasize a further statement, and to make it negative too.

comment [káment] v. 의견을 말하다; 논평하다; n. 의견; 언급
If you comment on something, you give your opinion about it or you give an explanation for it.

schedule [skédʒuːl] n. 일정, 스케줄
A schedule is a plan that gives a list of events or tasks and the times at which each one should happen or be done.

dedicate [dédikèit] v. (시간·노력을) 바치다, 전념[헌신]하다
(dedicated a. 전념하는, 헌신적인)
You use dedicated to describe someone who enjoys a particular activity very much and spends a lot of time doing it.

commit [kəmít] v. (일·활동 등에) 전념[헌신]하다 (committed a. 헌신적인, 열성적인)
If you commit yourself to something, you say that you will definitely do it.

1. Where did Arthur go to think about the jingle?

A. He went to the piano in his bedroom.

B. He went to the piano in the living room.

C. He went to the piano in the school music room.

D. He went to the piano in the music store.

2. What kind of bridge did Arthur have to cross in his dream?

A. A bridge with planks like piano keys

B. A bridge with planks like trumpet keys

C. A bridge with ropes like clarinet reeds

D. A bridge with ropes like guitar strings

3. What was D.W. doing in Arthur's dream?

A. She was writing a song for Arthur to use for the jingle.

B. She was pushing him across the bridge.

C. She was telling Arthur which notes to play.

D. She was standing on the other side of the bridge.

4. How did Arthur feel about D.W.'s song?

A. He thought it was perfect.

B. He thought it was funny.

C. He thought it was too simple.

D. He thought it was too complex.

5. What part of D.W.'s song did Arthur have to change?

A. He had to change the part about lunch.

B. He had to change the part about fun.

C. He had to change the part about Nadine.

D. He had to change the part about D.W.

Check Your Reading Speed

1분에 몇 단어를 읽는지 리딩 속도를 측정해보세요.

$$\frac{506\ \text{words}}{\text{reading time (\qquad) sec}} \times 60 = (\qquad)\ \text{WPM}$$

Build Your Vocabulary

복습 **knot** [nat] n. (긴장·화 등으로 복부·목 등이) 뻣뻣한 느낌; 매듭; v. 매듭을 묶다
If you feel a knot in your stomach, you get an uncomfortable tight feeling in your stomach, usually because you are afraid or excited.

★★ **tight** [tait] a. 팽팽한; 단단한; 조이는 듯한
If a part of your body is tight, it feels rather uncomfortable and painful, for example because you are ill, anxious, or angry.

★★ **comfortable** [kʌ́mfərtəbl] a. 편한, 안정된; 안락한, 쾌적한 (uncomfortable a. 불편한)
Something that is uncomfortable makes you feel slight pain or physical discomfort when you experience it or use it.

복습 **ignore** [ignɔ́:r] v. 무시하다, 모르는 체하다
If you ignore someone or something, you pay no attention to them.

hunch [hʌntʃ] v. (등을) 구부리다; n. 예감
If you hunch forward, you raise your shoulders, put your head down, and lean forward, often because you are cold, ill, or unhappy.

복습 **stare** [stɛər] v. 응시하다, 뚫어지게 보다
If you stare at someone or something, you look at them for a long time.

★★ **key** [ki:] n. (피아노) 건반; 열쇠; 수단
The keys of a piano or organ are the long narrow pieces of wood or plastic that you press in order to play it.

복습 **note** [nout] n. 음, 음표; 메모, 필기; 편지, 쪽지
In music, a note is the sound of a particular pitch, or a written symbol representing this sound.

★★ **hesitate** [hézətèit] v. 주저하다, 머뭇거리다, 망설이다
If you hesitate, you do not speak or act for a short time, usually because you are uncertain, embarrassed, or worried about what you are going to say or do.

★★ **groan** [groun] v. 신음하다, 끙끙거리다; n. 신음, 끙끙거리는 소리
If you groan, you make a long, low sound because you are in pain, or because you are upset or unhappy about something.

come up with idiom ~을 생각해 내다, ~을 내놓다
If you come up with a plan or idea, you think of it and suggest it.

jumble [dʒʌmbl] n. 뒤범벅, 뒤죽박죽 뒤섞인 것; 혼란
A jumble of things is a lot of different things that are all mixed together in a disorganized or confused way.

★ **chord** [kɔːrd] n. 코드, 화음; (악기의) 현; v. 가락이 맞다, 화음을 연주하다
A chord is a number of musical notes played or sung at the same time with a pleasing effect.

★★ **barely** [bέərli] ad. 간신히, 가까스로, 빠듯하게
You use barely to say that something is only just true or only just the case.

★ **gloom** [gluːm] n. 어둠; 우울, 침울
The gloom is a state of near darkness.

★★★ **part** [paːrt] v. 갈라지다, 벌어지다; 헤어지다
If things that are next to each other part or if you part them, they move in opposite directions, so that there is a space between them.

★ **reveal** [rivíːl] v. 나타내다, 보이다; 밝히다, 폭로하다
If you reveal something that has been out of sight, you uncover it so that people can see it.

creaky [kríːki] a. 삐걱거리는; 낡은
A creaky object makes short, high-pitched sound when it moves.

⁑ **bridge** [bridʒ] n. 다리, 교량; v. 다리를 놓다
A bridge is a structure that is built over a railway, river, or road so that people or vehicles can cross from one side to the other.

복습 **string** [striŋ] v. (strung–strung) 매달다, 묶다;
n. 끈, 실; (오케스트라의) 현악기부, 현악기 연주자들
If you string something somewhere, you hang it up between two or more objects.

⁎ **wooden** [wudn] a. 나무로 된, 목재의; 경직된
Wooden objects are made of wood.

⁎ **plank** [plæŋk] n. 널, 두꺼운 판자
A plank is a long, flat, rectangular piece of wood.

⁎ **sway** [swei] v. 흔들다, 흔들리다; (마음을) 흔들다; n. 흔들림
When people or things sway, they lean or swing slowly from one side to the other.

⁎ **secure** [sikjúər] a. 안전한, 튼튼한; 안심하는; v. 안전하게 지키다, 보호하다
If an object is secure, it is fixed firmly in position.

⁂ **pass** [pæs] n. 산길, 등산로; 합격, 통과; v. 지나가다; 통과하다 (mountain pass n. 산길)
A pass is a narrow path or route between mountains.

⁂ **cross** [krɔːs] v. 건너다, 가로지르다; 교차시키다; a. 가로지를; 교차한; n. 십자가
If you cross something such as a room, a road, or an area of land or water, you move or travel to the other side of it.

one way or the other idiom 어떻게 되든지
You can use one way or the other when you want to say that something definitely happens, but without giving any details about how it happens.

⁎ **frown** [fraun] v. 얼굴[눈살]을 찌푸리다; n. 찡그림, 찌푸림
When someone frowns, their eyebrows become drawn together, because they are annoyed or puzzled.

⋆ **leap** [li:p] n. 뜀, 도약; v. 껑충 뛰다; 뛰어넘다
If you take a leap, you jump high in the air or jump a long distance.

keep it up idiom 계속 노력하다, (일을) 계속 해나가다
You use keep it up when you tell someone to continue doing something as well as they are already doing it.

⋆ **hum** [hʌm] v. 콧노래를 부르다, (노래를) 흥얼거리다; 웅웅[윙윙]거리다
If something hums, it makes a low continuous noise.

복습 **tune** [tju:n] n. 곡조, 선율; v. 조율하다, 조정하다
A tune is a series of musical notes that is pleasant and easy to remember.

catchy [kǽʧi] a. 기억하기 쉬운
If you describe a tune, name, or advertisement as catchy, you mean that it is attractive and easy to remember.

⋆⋆ **beat** [bi:t] n. [음악] 박자; v. 치다, 두드리다; 패배시키다, 이기다
The beat of a piece of music is the main rhythm that it has.

⋆ **jerk** [dʒə:rk] ① v. 홱 움직이다; n. (갑자기 날카롭게) 홱 움직임 ② n. 바보, 멍청이
If you jerk something or someone in a particular direction, or they jerk in a particular direction, they move a short distance very suddenly and quickly.

복습 **hall** [hɔ:l] n. (건물의) 복도, 통로; 넓은 방[건물]; (건물 입구 안쪽의) 현관
A hall in a building is a long passage with doors into rooms on both sides of it.

upstairs [ʌ́pstɛ́ərz] n. 위층, 2층; ad. 위층으로, 위층에서
The upstairs of a building is the floor or floors that are higher than the ground floor.

tiptoe [típtòu] v. 발끝으로 살금살금 걷다; n. 발끝
If you tiptoe somewhere, you walk there very quietly without putting your heels on the floor when you walk.

peek [pi:k] v. 살짝 들여다보다, 엿보다; n. 엿봄
If you peek at something or someone, you have a quick look at them.

복습 **brush** [brʌʃ] v. 솔질을 하다; (솔이나 손으로) 털다
If you brush something or brush something such as dirt off it, you clean it or tidy it using a brush.

munch [mʌntʃ] v. 우적우적[아삭아삭] 먹다
If you munch food, you eat it by chewing it slowly, thoroughly, and rather noisily.

bulge [bʌldʒ] v. 툭 튀어 나오다; n. 툭 튀어 나온 것, 불룩한 것
If someone's eyes or veins are bulging, they seem to stick out a lot, often because the person is making a strong physical effort or is experiencing a strong emotion.

⁑ **race** [reis] ① v. 질주하다, 달리다; 경주하다; n. 경주 ② n. 인종, 민족
If you race somewhere, you go there as quickly as possible.

⁑ **downstairs** [dáunstέərz] ad. 아래층으로, 아래층에서; n. 아래층
If you go downstairs in a building, you go down a staircase toward the ground floor.

⁑ **spot** [spat] n. 장소, 지점; 얼룩, 반점; v. 발견하다, 분별하다
You can refer to a particular place as a spot.

⁑ **definite** [défənit] a. 확실한, 확고한; 분명한, 뚜렷한 (definitely ad. 확실히, 명확히)
If something such as a decision or an arrangement is definite, it is firm and clear, and unlikely to be changed.

lose one's mind idiom 미치다, 실성하다
If you say that someone is losing their mind, you mean that they are becoming mad.

복습 **crunch** [krʌntʃ] v. 아작아작[오도독] 씹다; n. 으드득 소리
If you crunch something hard, such as a sweet, you crush it noisily between your teeth.

out to lunch idiom 이상하게 행동하는, 미쳐서
If someone is out to lunch, they are crazy, stupid or confused.

1. What did Prunella say about Arthur and eating Crunch cereal?

A. She said that eating Crunch cereal may have rotted his ears.

B. She said that eating Crunch cereal may have rotted his stomach.

C. She said that eating Crunch cereal may have rotted his teeth.

D. She said that eating Crunch cereal may have rotted his brain.

2. How did Arthur say he was inspired?

A. He said that he had heard D.W. singing it.

B. He said that he had heard his dog, Pal, barking it.

C. He said that he heard the tune in his head and the words just came.

D. He said that he heard the tune on a TV commercial and added words.

3. How did the band feel about the jingle after lunch?

A. Everyone liked it.

B. Francine wanted to change the words.

C. Arthur wanted to sing the song alone.

D. Everyone still had problems with it.

4. What did the band do after they felt comfortable practicing?

A. Arthur used a CD recorder to record the song.

B. Arthur used a tape recorder to record the song.

C. Arthur used a computer to record the song.

D. Arthur used a camcorder to record a video of the song.

5. What was the good sign that Arthur saw?

A. Pal was jumping up and down in the yard.

B. Pal was running in circles in the yard.

C. Pal was barking loudly in the yard.

D. Pal was quietly eating food from his dish in the yard.

Check Your Reading Speed

1분에 몇 단어를 읽는지 리딩 속도를 측정해보세요.

$$\frac{520 \text{ words}}{\text{reading time (\qquad) sec}} \times 60 = (\qquad) \text{ WPM}$$

Build Your Vocabulary

★ **mood** [mu:d] n. 분위기, 기분
The mood of a place is the general impression that you get of it.

★ **grim** [grim] a. 암울한; 음산한; 엄숙한, 단호한
A place that is grim is unattractive and depressing in appearance.

복습 **garage** [gərá:dʒ] n. 차고, 주차장
A garage is a building in which you keep a car. A garage is often built next to or as part of a house.

★ **tap** [tæp] v. 톡톡 두드리다[치다]; (음악에 맞춰 손가락·발 등으로) 박자를 맞추다; n. 두드리기, 치기
If you tap something, you hit it with a quick light blow or a series of quick light blows.

★★★ **march** [ma:rʧ] ① n. 행진곡; 행군, 행진; v. 행진[행군]하다 (slow march n. 느린 행진곡) ② n. 3월
A march is a piece of music with a regular rhythm that you can march to.

warm up idiom 몸을 천천히 풀다, 준비 운동을 하다
If you warm up, you do gentle exercise or practice to prepare for exercise or a performance.

★★ **painful** [péinfəl] a. 괴로운, 골치 아픈; 아픈
Situations, memories, or experiences that are painful are difficult and unpleasant to deal with, and often make you feel sad and upset.

★ **screech** [skriːʧ] n. 끼익; 빽; v. 끼익 하는 소리를 내다
A screech is a loud, unpleasant, high-pitched noise.

★ **accidental** [æksədéntl] a. 우연한; 돌발적인 (accidentally ad. 우연히)
An accidental event happens by chance or as the result of an accident, and is not deliberately intended.

★ **tail** [teil] n. 꼬리; (동전의) 뒷면; v. 미행하다
The tail of an animal, bird, or fish is the part extending beyond the end of its body.

run out idiom (시간·돈 등이) 없어지다; (물자 등이) 다 떨어지다, 다하다
If something runs out, it is finished or used up.

복습 **spot** [spat] n. 지점, 장소; 얼룩, 반점; v. 발견하다, 분별하다
You can refer to a particular place as a spot.

put aside idiom ~을 한쪽으로 치우다
If you put something aside, you place it to one side.

★★ **doubt** [daut] n. 의심, 의혹, 의문; v. 확신하지 못하다, 의문[의혹]을 갖다
If you have doubt or doubts about something, you feel uncertain about it and do not know whether it is true or possible.

wail [weil] v. (길고 높은) 소리를 내다; 통곡하다, 흐느끼다; n. 울부짖음, 통곡
If something such as a siren or an alarm wails, it makes a long, loud, high-pitched sound.

let down idiom 실망시키다, 낙심시키다; 낮추다, 내리다
If you let down someone, you disappoint them by failing to do what you agreed to do or were expected to do.

★ **rot** [rat] v. 썩다, 썩히다, 부식시키다; n. 썩음, 부식, 부패
When food, wood, or another substance rots, or when something rots it, it becomes softer and is gradually destroyed.

make a face idiom 얼굴을 찌푸리다, 침울한 표정을 짓다
If you make a face, you twist your face to indicate a certain mental or emotional state.

ooze [u:z] v. 스며 나오다, 새어 나오다; n. 스며 나옴
When a thick or sticky liquid oozes from something or when something oozes it, the liquid flows slowly and in small quantities.

★★ **rush** [rʌʃ] v. 급히 움직이다, 서두르다, 돌진하다
If people rush to do something, they do it as soon as they can, because they are very eager to do it.

복습 **jingle** [dʒiŋgl] n. (라디오·텔레비전의) 시엠송(광고방송용 노래); 딸랑, 짤랑
A jingle is a short, simple tune, often with words, which is used to advertise a product or program on radio or television.

★★★ **still** [stil] a. 조요한, 고요한; 정지한, 움직이지 않는; ad. 여전히, 아직도
If a place is still, it is quiet and shows no sign of activity.

복습 **hunch** [hʌntʃ] n. 예감; v. (등을) 구부리다
If you have a hunch about something, you are sure that it is correct or true, even though you do not have any proof.

복습 **munch** [mʌntʃ] v. 우적우적[아삭아삭] 먹다
If you munch food, you eat it by chewing it slowly, thoroughly, and rather noisily.

복습 **beat** [bi:t] n. [음악] 박자; v. 치다, 두드리다; 패배시키다, 이기다
The beat of a piece of music is the main rhythm that it has.

복습 **snap** [snæp] v. 손가락을 튕기다; 홱 움직이다; 딱[툭] (하고) 부러뜨리다; n. 딱[탁] 하는 소리
(snap one's fingers idiom 손가락으로 딱 소리를 내다)
If you snap your fingers, you make a sharp sound by moving your middle finger quickly across your thumb, for example in order to accompany music or to order someone to do something.

★ **clap** [klæp] v. 박수를 치다; n. 박수(소리)
When you clap, you hit your hands together to show appreciation or attract attention.

way to go idiom 잘했어
People say 'way to go!' to encourage someone to continue the good work.

복습 **inspire** [inspáiər] v. 영감을 주다; 고무하다, 격려하다; (감정 등을) 불어넣다
If someone or something inspires you, they give you new ideas and a strong feeling of enthusiasm.

복습 **explain** [ikspléin] v. 설명하다, 분명하게 하다
If you explain something, you give details about it or describe it so that it can be understood.

복습 **inspiration** [ìnspəréiʃən] n. 영감, 기발한 생각
Inspiration is a feeling of enthusiasm you get from someone or something, which gives you new and creative ideas.

복습 **tune** [tjuːn] n. 곡조, 선율; v. 조율하다, 조정하다
A tune is a series of musical notes that is pleasant and easy to remember.

복습 **pause** [pɔːz] v. (말·일을 하다가) 잠시 멈추다; n. (말·행동 등의) 멈춤
If you pause while you are doing something, you stop for a short period and then continue.

★★ **lower** [louər] v. 낮추다, 내리다
If you lower something, you move it slowly downward.

★ **fiddle** [fidl] v. 만지작거리다; 바이올린을 켜다; n. 바이올린
If you fiddle with an object, you keep moving it or touching it with your fingers.

복습 **impress** [imprés] v. 깊은 인상을 주다, 감명을 주다 (impressed a. 감명을 받은)
If something impresses you, you feel great admiration for it.

poof [puːf] int. 휙, 팟
Some people say poof to indicate that something happened very suddenly.

out of nowhere idiom 어디선지 모르게, 갑자기
If something comes or happens out of nowhere, it comes from an unknown place or happens suddenly or unexpectedly.

bite [bait] v. (bit-bitten) (이빨로) 물다, 베어 물다; n. 물기; 한 입
If you bite something, you use your teeth to cut into it, for example in order to eat it or break it.

hand [hænd] v. 건네주다, 넘겨주다; n. 손, 도움(의 손길)
If you hand something to someone, you pass it to them.

sheet music [ʃi:t mjú:zik] n. 한 곡 단위로 인쇄한 악보
Sheet music is music that is printed on sheets of paper without a hard cover.

grin [grin] v. (이를 드러내고) 싱긋 웃다, 활짝 웃다; n. 싱긋 웃음
When you grin, you smile broadly.

practice [prǽktis] v. 연습하다; 실행하다; n. 연습, 훈련; 실행, 실천
If you practice something, you keep doing it regularly in order to be able to do it better.

comfortable [kʌ́mfərtəbl] a. 편한, 안정된; 안락한, 쾌적한
If you feel comfortable with a particular situation or person, you feel confident and relaxed with them.

set up idiom (기계·장비를) 설치하다; ~을 세우다, 놓다
If you set up a machine or equipment, you make them ready to use.

tape recorder [teip rikɔ́:rdər] n. 테이프 리코더, 녹음기
A tape recorder is a machine used for recording and playing music, speech, or other sounds.

nod [nad] v. (고개를) 끄덕이다, 끄덕여 나타내다; n. (고개를) 끄덕임, 까딱거림
If you nod, you move your head downward and upward to show agreement, understanding, or approval.

복습 **yard** [jaːrd] n. 마당, 뜰
A yard is a piece of land next to someone's house, with grass and plants growing in it.

복습 **sign** [sain] n. 징후, 흔적; 표지판, 표시; v. 서명하다; 신호를 보내다
If there is a sign of something, there is something which shows that it exists or is happening.

1. What did Arthur promise everyone in the band as they left?

A. He promised to share the money equally among the members.

B. He promised to let everyone know as soon as he heard anything.

C. He promised everyone that they would definitely win the contest.

D. He promised everyone a copy of the recording of the song.

2. What did D.W. want Arthur to do for her?

A. She wanted Arthur to let her listen to the jingle.

B. She wanted Arthur to give her Crunch cereal.

C. She wanted Arthur to write her name on the entry form.

D. She wanted Arthur to make another recording with her.

3. Why did Arthur think there was no reason to tell D.W. about the jingle?

A. D.W. would never hear about the jingle.

B. Nobody could really own a jingle.

C. Great artists always took inspiration from the people and places around them.

D. D.W. had already given him permission to use her song.

4. What happened to D.W. in Arthur's daydream?

A. She was booed off stage by Arthur's fans in the audience.

B. She told everyone on stage the truth about Arthur's song.

C. She reached the stage and pushed Arthur away from the piano.

D. She tried to make it to the stage but was blocked by security.

5. How did Arthur feel at the mailbox?

A. He smiled and quickly dropped the envelope in the mailbox.

B. He sighed and hesitated dropping the envelope in the mailbox.

C. He frowned and put the envelope back in his coat pocket.

D. He thought bringing it to the post office would be faster.

Check Your Reading Speed

1분에 몇 단어를 읽는지 리딩 속도를 측정해보세요.

$$\frac{534 \text{ words}}{\text{reading time (\qquad) sec}} \times 60 = (\qquad) \text{ WPM}$$

Build Your Vocabulary

★★ **prize** [práiz] n. 상(품); 경품; v. 소중하게 여기다

A prize is money or something valuable that is given to someone who has the best results in a competition or game, or as a reward for doing good work.

복습 **include** [inklú:d] v. ~을 포함하다, (~에) 포함시키다

If one thing includes another thing, it has the other thing as one of its parts.

★★ **flexible** [fléksəbl] a. 융통성 있는; 잘 구부러지는, 유연한

Something or someone that is flexible is able to change easily and adapt to different conditions and circumstances as they occur.

toot [tu:t] v. (나팔 등) 관악기를 불다; 경적을 울리다

If someone toots an instrument, they blowsand sound it.

★★★ **twice** [twais] a. 두 번; 두 배로

If something happens twice, there are two actions or events of the same kind.

★★ **package** [pǽkidʒ] n. 소포; 포장물

A package is something wrapped in paper, usually so that it can be sent to someone by post.

복습 **envelope** [énvəlòup] n. 봉투

An envelope is the rectangular paper cover in which you send a letter to someone through the post.

figure out idiom (양·비용을) 계산하다, ~을 알아내다
If you figure out a solution to a problem or the reason for something, you succeed in solving it or understanding it.

☆☆ **stamp** [stæmp] n. 우표; 인지; 도장; v. (도장·스탬프 등을) 찍다; (발을) 구르다
A stamp or a postage stamp is a small piece of paper which you lick and stick on an envelope or package before you post it to pay for the cost of the postage.

복습 **spot** [spat] v. 발견하다, 분별하다; n. 장소, 지점; 얼룩, 반점
If you spot something or someone, you notice them.

복습 **jingle** [dʒiŋgl] n. (라디오·텔레비전의) 시엠송(광고방송용 노래); 딸랑, 짤랑
A jingle is a short, simple tune, often with words, which is used to advertise a product or program on radio or television.

복습 **contest** [kántest] n. 대회, 시합; v. 경쟁을 벌이다, 다투다
A contest is a competition or game in which people try to win.

복습 **come up with** idiom ~을 생각해내다, ~을 내놓다
If you come up with a plan or idea, you think of it and suggest it.

☆☆☆ **polite** [pəláit] a. 예의 바른, 공손한
Someone who is polite has good manners and behaves in a way that is socially correct and not rude to other people.

put words in a person's mouth idiom (말도 안 한 것을) 말하였다고 하다
If someone puts words in your mouth, they say or suggest that you have said something, when you have not.

복습 **frown** [fraun] v. 얼굴[눈살]을 찌푸리다; n. 찡그림, 찌푸림
When someone frowns, their eyebrows become drawn together, because they are annoyed or puzzled.

복습 **munch** [mʌntʃ] v. 우적우적[아삭아삭] 먹다
If you munch food, you eat it by chewing it slowly, thoroughly, and rather noisily.

복습 **crunch** [krʌntʃ] v. 아작아작[오도독] 씹다; n. 으드득 소리
If you crunch something hard, such as a sweet, you crush it noisily between your teeth.

복습 **snap** [snæp] n. 딱[탁] 하는 소리; v. 홱 움직이다; 손가락을 튕기다; 딱[툭] (하고) 부러뜨리다
A snap is a sharp cracking noise.

crackle [krækl] n. (짧고 날카롭게) 탁탁하는 소리; v. 탁탁[치직] 소리를 내다
A crackle is a rapid series of short, harsh noises.

★ **pop** [pap] n. 뻥[탁] 하는 소리; 발포; v. 불쑥 나타나다; 뻥 하고 터뜨리다
Pop is a short sharp sound, for example the sound made by bursting a balloon or by pulling a cork out of a bottle.

★★ **miss** [mis] v. (늦게 도착하여) ~을 놓치다; (치거나 잡거나 닿지 못하고) 놓치다; ~을 빠뜨리다
If you miss something such as a plane or train, you arrive too late to catch it.

more than a little idiom 상당히, 적지 않게
If you are more than a little excited or shocked, you are quite or very excited or shocked.

복습 **strange** [streindʒ] a. 이상한, 낯선
Something that is strange is unusual or unexpected, and makes you feel slightly nervous or afraid.

★ **shrug** [ʃrʌg] v. (양 손바닥을 내보이면서 어깨를) 으쓱하다; n. (어깨를) 으쓱하기
If you shrug, you raise your shoulders to show that you are not interested in something or that you do not know or care about something.

contagious [kəntéidʒəs] a. 전염되는, 전염성의
A disease that is contagious can be caught by touching people or things that are infected with it.

★★ **avoid** [əvɔ́id] v. 피하다, 막다; 모면하다
If you avoid something unpleasant that might happen, you take action in order to prevent it from happening.

복습 **inspiration** [ìnspəréiʃən] n. 영감, 기발한 생각
Inspiration is a feeling of enthusiasm you get from someone or something, which gives you new and creative ideas.

★★ **cheer** [ʧiər] v. 환호성을 지르다, 응원하다; n. 환호(성)
When people cheer, they shout loudly to show their approval or to encourage someone who is doing something such as taking part in a game.

★★★ **crowd** [kraud] n. 군중, 인파; 많은 것, 다수; v. 모여들다, 붐비다
A crowd is a large group of people who have gathered together, for example to watch or listen to something interesting, or to protest about something.

★★ **theme** [θiːm] n. 주제, 테마; a. 특정 분위기를 살린
A theme in a piece of writing, a talk, or a discussion is an important idea or subject that runs through it.

복습 **flash** [flæʃ] v. (미소 등을 남에게) 얼른 보내다; 번쩍 비추다; 휙 지나가다; n. 순간; 번쩍임
If you flash a look or a smile at someone, you suddenly look at them or smile at them.

복습 **grin** [grin] n. 싱긋 웃음; v. (이를 드러내고) 싱긋 웃다, 활짝 웃다
A grin is a broad smile.

★★ **row** [rou] ① n. 열, 줄; 좌석 줄 ② v. 노[배]를 젓다
A row of things or people is a number of them arranged in a line.

climb [klaim] v. 오르다, 올라가다; n. 등산, 등반
If you climb something such as a tree, mountain, or ladder, or climb up it, you move toward the top of it.

복습 **rush** [rʌʃ] v. 급히 움직이다, 서두르다, 돌진하다
If people rush to do something, they do it as soon as they can, because they are very eager to do it.

★★★ **block** [blak] v. (길 등을) 막다, 방해하다; n. 덩어리, 블록
If you block someone's way, you prevent them from going somewhere or entering a place by standing in front of them.

beefy [bí:fi] a. 우람한, 뚱뚱한
Someone, especially a man, who is beefy has a big body and large muscles.

*** **head** [hed] n. (단체 · 조직의) 책임자; 머리, 고개; v. (특정 방향으로) 가다
The head of a company or organization is the person in charge of it and in charge of the people in it.

* **security** [sikjúərəti] n. 보안, 경비; 경비 담당 부서
Security refers to all the measures that are taken to protect a place, or to ensure that only people with permission enter it or leave it.

* **determined** [ditə́:rmind] a. 단호한, 완강한; 단단히 결심한
If you are determined to do something, you have made a firm decision to do it and will not let anything stop you.

복습 **sigh** [sai] v. 한숨 쉬다; n. 한숨, 탄식
When you sigh, you let out a deep breath, as a way of expressing feelings such as disappointment, tiredness, or pleasure.

* **mailbox** [méilbàks] n. 우편함, 우체통
A mailbox is a metal box in a public place, where you put letters and packets to be collected.

nothing to it idiom 손쉬운 일이다, 아주 쉽다
If you say there's nothing to it, you mean that it is easy to do.

복습 **blink** [bliŋk] v. 눈을[눈이] 깜박이다; n. 눈을 깜빡거림
When you blink or when you blink your eyes, you shut your eyes and very quickly open them again.

1. What were Arthur and D.W. doing on a Saturday morning two weeks later?

A. They were watching TV.

B. They were eating breakfast.

C. They were playing with toys.

D. They were doing their homework.

2. How did D.W. react to the Crunch commercial?

A. She did not notice that it was her song.

B. She was excited to hear her song on TV.

C. She thought it seemed better than the old one.

D. She wanted an explanation from Arthur.

3. How did the delivery man appear when he arrived at Arthur's home?

A. He was driving a car shaped like a Crunch cereal piece.

B. He was wearing a hat shaped like a bowl of cereal.

C. He was wearing glasses shaped like bowls of cereal.

D. He was wearing a tie with Crunch cereal designs.

4. Whose name was written on the certificate?

A. Mr. and Mrs. Read

B. Mr. Arthur Read

C. Ms. D.W. Read

D. The Crunch Bunch band

5. How did Mr. and Mrs. Read react to Arthur and D.W. throwing snowballs at each other?

A. They tried to stop them and asked them to come inside.

B. They joined in with them to throw snowballs at each other.

C. They told them not to hit the boxes of Crunch cereal with snow.

D. They left them to do it in order to work up their appetites.

Check Your Reading Speed

1분에 몇 단어를 읽는지 리딩 속도를 측정해보세요.

$$\frac{\text{631 words}}{\text{reading time (\qquad) sec}} \times 60 = (\qquad) \text{ WPM}$$

Build Your Vocabulary

pajama [pədʒá:mə] n. (pl.) 파자마, 잠옷
A pair of pajamas consists of loose trousers and a loose jacket that people wear in bed.

★ **defeat** [difí:t] v. 물리치다, 이기다, 패배시키다; n. 패배; 타도, 타파
If you defeat someone, you win a victory over them in a battle, game, or contest.

복습 **commercial** [kəmə́:rʃəl] n. (텔레비전·라디오의) 광고; a. 상업의, 무역의
A commercial is an advertisement that is broadcast on television or radio.

have one's hands full idiom 아주 바쁘다, 손에 꽉 찼다
If you have your hands full with something, you are very busy because of it.

복습 **hunch** [hʌntʃ] n. 예감; v. (등을) 구부리다
If you have a hunch about something, you are sure that it is correct or true, even though you do not have any proof.

tuxedo [tʌksí:dou] n. 턱시도
A tuxedo is a black or white jacket worn by men for formal social events.

복습 **microphone** [máikrəfòun] n. 마이크(로폰)
A microphone is a device that is used to make sounds louder or to record them on a tape recorder.

복습 **munch** [mʌntʃ] v. 우적우적[아삭아삭] 먹다
If you munch food, you eat it by chewing it slowly, thoroughly, and rather noisily.

* **yawn** [jɔːn] v. 하품하다; n. 하품
If you yawn, you open your mouth very wide and breathe in more air than usual, often when you are tired or when you are not interested in something.

복습 **race** [reis] ① v. 질주하다, 달리다; 경주하다; n. 경주 ② n. 인종, 민족
If you race somewhere, you go there as quickly as possible.

복습 **explain** [ikspléin] v. 설명하다, 분명하게 하다
If you explain something, you give details about it or describe it so that it can be understood.

calm down idiom (노여움·흥분을) 가라앉히다
If you calm down, or if someone calms you down, you become less angry, upset, or excited.

* **poke** [pouk] v. 쑥 내밀다; (손가락 등으로) 쿡 찌르다; n. 찌르기, 쑤시기
If you poke your head through an opening or if it pokes through an opening, you push it through, often so that you can see something more easily.

* **fiber** [fáibər] n. (식품의) 섬유소, 섬유질
Fiber consists of the parts of plants or seeds that your body cannot digest.

복습 **bowl** [boul] n. 그릇, 사발
A bowl is a round container with a wide uncovered top.

industrial-strength [indʌ́striəl-stréŋθ] a. 아주 강한, 강력한
If a product is industrial-strength, it is much stronger or more powerful than the product normally available to use.

복습 **entry** [éntri] n. 응모권; 참가, 출입; 입장, 등장
An entry for a competition is a piece of work, for example a story or drawing, or the answers to a set of questions, which you complete in order to take part in the competition.

do something over idiom ~을 다시 하다
If you do something over, you do it again or start doing it again from the beginning.

★ **convince** [kənvíns] v. 확신시키다, 납득시키다; 설득하다 (convinced a. 확신하는)
If someone or something convinces you of something, they make you believe that it is true or that it exists.

★★★ **lose** [lu:z] v. 실패하다; 지다; (기회를) 놓치다
If you lose a contest, a fight, or an argument, you do not succeed because someone does better than you and defeats you.

roll one's eyes idiom 눈을 굴리다
If you roll your eyes, you show with your eyes that you don't believe someone or aren't interested in what they're saying.

make sense idiom 뜻이 통하다; 도리에 맞다
If something makes sense, it has a meaning that you can easily understand.

복습 **stuff** [stʌf] n. 것(들), 물건, 물질; v. 채워 넣다, 채우다
You can use stuff to refer to things such as a substance, a collection of things, events, or ideas, or the contents of something in a general way without mentioning the thing itself by name.

복습 **tap** [tæp] v. 톡톡 두드리다[치다]; (음악에 맞춰 손가락·발 등으로) 박자를 맞추다; n. 두드리기[치기]
If you tap something, you hit it with a quick light blow or a series of quick light blows.

복습 **contest** [kántest] n. 대회, 시합; v. 경쟁을 벌이다, 다투다
A contest is a competition or game in which people try to win.

interrupt [ìntərʌ́pt] v. 중단하다, 가로막다, 저지하다
If you interrupt someone who is speaking, you say or do something that causes them to stop.

delivery [dilívəri] n. (물품 · 편지 등의) 배달 (delivery man n. 배달원)
Delivery or a delivery is the bringing of letters, parcels, or other goods to someone's house or to another place where they want them.

residence [rézədəns] n. 거주지; 거주, 상주
Your place of residence is the place where you live.

cautious [kɔ́:ʃəs] a. 조심스러운, 신중한 (cautiously ad. 조심스럽게)
Someone who is cautious acts very carefully in order to avoid possible danger.

throat [θrout] n. 목구멍; 목 (clear one's throat idiom 목을 가다듬다, 헛기침하다)
Your throat is the back of your mouth and the top part of the tubes that go down into your stomach and your lungs.

on behalf of idiom ~을 대표하여, 대신하여
If you do something on behalf of someone, you do it for that person as their representative.

present [prizént] v. 선물하다, 증정하다; 건네주다, 내놓다; n. 선물
If you present someone with something such as a prize or document, or if you present it to them, you formally give it to them.

supply [səplái] n. 공급(량), 비축(량); v. 공급하다, 제공하다
A supply of something is an amount of it which someone has or which is available for them to use.

motion [móuʃən] v. 몸짓으로 알리다; n. 운동, 동작
If you motion to someone, you move your hand or head as a way of telling them to do something or telling them where to go.

crate [kreit] n. 나무 상자, (짐을 보호하는) 나무틀
A crate is a large box used for transporting or storing things.

driveway [dráivwèi] n. (도로에서 집·차고까지의) 진입로, 차도
A driveway is a piece of hard ground that leads from the road to the front of a house or other building.

⋆ **certificate** [sərtífikət] n. 증서, 증명서; 자격증
A certificate is an official document stating that particular facts are true.

⋆ **proclaim** [proukléim] v. 공포하다, 선언하다, 성명하다
If people proclaim something, they formally make it known to the public.

⋆ **winner** [wínər] n. 우승자, 승자
The winner of a prize, race, or competition is the person, animal, or thing that wins it.

복습 **jingle** [dʒiŋgl] n. (라디오·텔레비전의) 시엠송(광고방송용 노래); 딸랑, 짤랑
A jingle is a short, simple tune, often with words, which is used to advertise a product or program on radio or television.

⋆ **overwhelm** [òuvərhwélm] v. 압도하다, 제압하다 (overwhelmed a. 어쩔 줄 모르는)
If you are overwhelmed by a feeling or event, it affects you very strongly, and you do not know how to deal with it.

복습 **sigh** [sai] v. 한숨 쉬다; n. 한숨, 탄식
When you sigh, you let out a deep breath, as a way of expressing feelings such as disappointment, tiredness, or pleasure.

⋆⋆ **gather** [gǽðər] v. 모이다, 집결하다; 모으다, 끌다
If people gather somewhere or if someone gathers people somewhere, they come together in a group.

get one's hopes up idiom ~에게 희망을 품게 하다
If you tell someone not to get their hopes up, you are warning them that they should not become too confident of progress or success.

crummy [krʌ́mi] a. 형편없는, 초라한
Something that is crummy is unpleasant, of very poor quality, or not good enough.

★ **beam** [bi:m] v. 활짝 웃다; 비추다; n. 환한 얼굴; 기둥; 빛줄기
If you say that someone is beaming, you mean that they have a big smile on their face because they are happy, pleased, or proud about something.

stink [stiŋk] v. (고약한) 냄새가 나다, 악취가 풍기다; n. 악취
To stink means to smell extremely unpleasant.

★ **breeze** [bri:z] n. 산들바람, 미풍; v. 산들산들 불다
A breeze is a gentle wind.

★★ **chase** [ʧeis] v. 뒤쫓다, 추적하다; 재촉하다; n. 추적, 추격
If you chase someone, or chase after them, you run after them or follow them quickly in order to catch or reach them.

step on idiom ~을 (짓)밟다
If you step on something, you place or press your foot on it.

pelt [pelt] v. (무엇을 던지며) 공격하다, 퍼붓다
If you pelt someone with things, you throw things at them.

★ **appetite** [ǽpətàit] n. 식욕, 욕구
Your appetite is your desire to eat.

★★★ **firm** [fə:rm] ① a. 굳은, 단단한; 견고한 (firmly ad. 굳게) ② n. 회사
If something is firm, it does not shake or move when you put weight or pressure on it, because it is strongly made or securely fastened.

본문에 나온 악기들

banjo
cello
clarinet
Pearl
drum
harmonica
kazoo
oboe
piccolo
saxsophone
trumpet
tuba
violin

1장

page 5

"시나몬 살짝... 갈색설탕 약간... 그리고 정향을 아주 조금."

리드 씨는 가스레인지 앞에 서서, 그의 가장 최근의 작품에 생명을 불어넣고 있었습니다. 냄비에서 나오는 김이 서리가 낀 창문을 향해 소용돌이치며 올라갔습니다.

"그래, 그렇고말고. 오늘 같이 싸늘한 아침에는, 모두들 확실히 허기를 채워줄 오트밀을 먹어야 해."

page 6

그는 재빨리 빙글 돌아서 김이 나는 냄비를 내보였습니다.

나머지 가족들은 테이블에 앉아 있었습니다.

"저는 오늘 아침에는 별로 배고프지 않아요." 아서가 말했습니다.

"저도 안 고파요." D.W.가 말했습니다.

오직 아기 케이트만이 기뻐하는 것처럼 보였습니다. 그녀는 오트밀을 가지고 노는 것을 좋아했습니다. 그것은 항상 가장 흥미로운 장소에서 끝났습니다.

"자, 자." 엄마가 말했습니다. "너희 아빠가 열심히 만드셨잖니. 기회를 한번 드리자꾸나."

"고마워요, 여보." 리드 씨가 말했습니다. "그리고 당신의 지지에 대한 보답으로 맛있고 건강에 좋은 당신의 몫부터 시작해 보죠."

그는 냄비를 기울여서 그녀의 그릇에 조금 담으려고 했습니다. 하지만 아무것도 나오지 않았습니다. 오트밀은 마치 시멘트처럼 굳어 있었습니다.

page 7

"흠..." 리드 씨는 당황한 듯이 보였습니다. "베이킹 소다가 당밀과 반응한 게 틀림없어..."

"그것 참 안 됐네요!" 리드 부인이 말했습니다. 그렇지만 그녀의 표정에서는 그녀가 전혀 걱정하는 것처럼 보이지 않았습니다.

"큰일 *날 뻔* 했어." D.W.가 속삭였습니다.

아서는 고개를 끄덕였습니다.

"우리 아무래도 일반 시리얼로 때워야겠구나." 리드 부인이 말했습니다. "아서, 네가—"

"그럼요, 엄마!" 아서는 찬장에서 시리얼을 가져오기 위해 일어섰습니다.

리드 씨는 냄비를 싱크대에 놓았습니다. "우리 이것을 나중에 묻어야겠다— 물론, 완전한 예를 갖추고 말이야."

아서는 크런치 시리얼 상자를 열었습니다. 그것은 그가 가장 좋아하는 것이었습니다.

page 8

아빠는 고개를 저었습니다. "나는 저

설탕옷을 입힌 마분지의 매력을 이해할 수가 없어. 내 말을 믿으렴, 네가 거기서 얻을 수 있는 모든 것은 한 입 가득한 충치뿐일 거야."

"우리는 그 위험을 기꺼이 감수하겠어요." D.W.가 말했습니다.

아서가 먹을 분량을 털어내자, 편지 봉투가 상자에서 나와 그의 접시로 떨어졌습니다.

"와!" D.W.가 말했습니다. "나는 편지들이 알파벳 수프에만 들어 있는 거라고 생각했어."

아서는 봉투를 열고 안에 들어 있던 쪽지를 크게 읽었습니다.

"크런치 시리얼 로고송 콘테스트에 온 것을 환영합니다. 당신의 노래를 보내주세요. 그러면 1년 치 분량의 크런치 시리얼을 탈 수 있습니다."

리드 씨는 고개를 저었습니다. "2등상은 틀림없이 2년 치 시리얼이겠지."

아서는 계속 읽었습니다.

page 10

"우승한 노래는 또한 새 크런치 시리얼 광고로 TV에 방영이 될 것입니다. 그러니 거기 가만히 서있지 마시고, 와그작거리기 시작하세요."

"만약 우리가 우승한다면," D.W.가 말했습니다. "우린 유명해질 거야!"

"여기에 작은 글씨로 뭔가 있어." 아서가 말했습니다. "'각 응모는 20개의 상자 뚜껑과 함께'" 그는 한숨 쉬었습니다. "정말 많이 와그작거려야겠는데."

"거기 '법률로 금지한 곳에서는 무효'라고 쓰여 있지는 않니?" 리드 씨가 물었습니다.

아서가 보았습니다. "그런 것 같지는 않은데요." 그가 말했습니다.

"좋았어." D.W.가 말했습니다.

아서는 그녀의 접시 위에 시리얼을 부었습니다. "네가 그렇게 느낀다니 기뻐. 만약 네가 유명해지고 싶다면, 먹기 시작해."

2장

page 11

그 후로 며칠 동안, 아서는 양치질을 하는 동안 로고송에 대해 생각했습니다.

와그작, 와그작.

그는 목욕을 하는 동안에도 그것에 대해 생각했습니다.

와그작, 와그작, 와그작.

그는 심지어 숙제를 하면서도 그것에 대해 생각했습니다.

와그작, 와그작, 와그작, 와그작.

하지만 이런 생각 중 어느 것도 그를 진전시키지 않았습니다. 로고송을 쓰고 싶다고 생각하는 것은 그것을 실제로 만드는 것보다 훨씬 쉬웠습니다.

page 12

"아서, 너 신선한 공기를 좀 마실 필요가 있겠구나." 엄마가 말했습니다. "밖에 나가서 좀 놀아라."

"그럴 수 없어요, 엄마. 마감기한이 다가오고 있어요."

"가끔은, 잠시 휴식을 취하는 것이 좋단다." 리드 부인이 말했습니다. "네 창의력 배터리를 재충전하렴. 머릿속을 비워. 나가서 눈사람을 만들어 보는 것은 어떠니?"

"저는 그렇게 생각하—"

"움직여!" 엄마가 말했습니다. "이건 명령이야."

아서는 밖으로 나갔지만, 그것은 행복하지 않았습니다. 그는 큰 눈덩이를 굴리기 시작했습니다. 그리고 그는 그것을 조금씩 깎아내기 시작했습니다.

눈덩이는 큰 조각의 크런치 시리얼처럼 보이기 시작했습니다.

"이거 내가 생각하는 그거 맞지?"

D.W.도 밖으로 나와 있었습니다. 그녀는 아서의 눈 조각상을 보고 고개를 저었습니다.

"엄마는 내가 머릿속을 비우길 원하셔." 그가 설명했습니다. "난 이게 도움이 되길 바랐어."

page14

"오빠는 틀에 빠진 거야." D.W.가 말했습니다. "오빠는 더 열심히 생각할 필요가 있어."

"나 노력하고 있어." 아서가 주장했습니다. "난 내 인생에서 이렇게 열심히 생각해 본 적이 없어."

"글쎄, 그게 별로 드러나고 있지 않잖아. 어쩌면 내가 도와줄 수도 있겠다."

"우리 이것에 대해 이미 결정했잖아, D.W. 넌 네 일이 있어."

"알아, 알아. 난 시리얼을 먹기로 되어 있지."

아서가 고개를 끄덕였습니다. "그 사실을 잊지 마."

"잊어?" D.W.가 말했습니다. "어떻게 내가 잊겠어? 오빠가 내 침대, 장난감 상자, 그리고 내 옷장에 상자들을 두었잖아. 내가 가는 모든 곳에서, 크런치 시리얼이 나를 기다리고 있는 걸."

"불평하지 마." 아서가 말했습니다. "나도 먹고 있다고. 그리고 나는 여전히 해결해야 할 어려운 부분을 맡고 있어."

D.W.는 감명 받지 않았습니다. "오빤 제대로 해내고 있는 것 같아 보이지 않아. 오빠 *dunce*는 시도해 봤어? 그거 *크런치*랑 어느 정도 운율이 맞잖아."

page 15

"어느 정도라고? 난 크런치 시리얼 회사 사람들이 *어느 정도*를 찾는다고 생각하지 않아. 그 사람들은 리듬을 찾고 있어. 그 사람들은 시를 찾고 있—"

"그 사람들은 시리얼을 더 많이 팔 방

법을 찾는 거야." D.W.가 말했습니다.

아서는 고개를 저었습니다. "넌 좋은 태도를 갖고 있지 않아. 놀랄 일도 아니지. 넌 위대한 예술을 이해하기에 너무 어려."

D.W.는 웃음을 터뜨렸습니다. "내가 위대한 예술을 모를지는 몰라도, 내가 뭘 좋아하는지는 알아."

"우린 지금 아이스크림 맛에 대해서 이야기하고 있는 게 아니잖아, D.W. 로고송은 완벽한 멜로디와 함께 단어의 완벽한 조합이어야만 해."

"그럼, *lunch*는 어때?" D.W.가 말했습니다. "그건 *크런치*랑 운율이 맞잖아."

아서는 하늘을 올려다보고 한숨을 쉬었습니다. 왜 영감이 번쩍하는 번개처럼 그에게 내리지 않는 것일까요? 그는 준비가 되었습니다. 그는 기다리고 있었습니다.

page 16

눈뭉치가 그의 가슴을 쳤습니다.

"명중이오!" D.W.가 외쳤습니다.

"나도 곧바로 너를 명중시켜 주겠어!" 아서가 말했습니다.

그는 눈을 조금 떠서 반대로 던졌습니다.

적어도 잠시 동안은 그의 머릿속이 비었습니다.

3장

page 17

학교 음악실은 아서를 제외하고는 비어 있었습니다. 다른 모든 아이들은 쉬는 시간에 밖으로 나가서, 뛰어다니며 눈 속에서 놀고 있었습니다.

아서는 음을 피아노로 치고 있었습니다.

둥!

너무 낮아, 아서가 생각했습니다. 너무 슬퍼.

그는 높은 음을 쳐봤습니다.

딕.

너무 바보 같아, 아서가 생각했습니다.

그는 사이에 있는 음을 쳤습니다.

딩.

아서가 고개를 끄덕였습니다. 그것이 시작이었습니다.

page 18

음악실의 문이 쾅 하고 열렸습니다.

"네 로고송 어떻게 되고 있니, 아서?" 버스터가 물었습니다. 그의 얼굴은 빨갰습니다. 녹고 있는 눈이 그의 코트에서 졸졸 떨어지고 있었습니다.

"나 가사는 거의 다 끝냈어."

"어디 들어 보자." 버스터가 말했습니다.

아서는 목청을 가다듬었습니다.

"크런치를 먹어요." 그가 말했습니다.

버스터는 기다렸습니다. 하지만 아서는 다 끝낸 것처럼 보였습니다.

"더 있어?" 그가 물었습니다.

"아니, 이게 다야." 아서가 말했습니다. "어떻게 생각해?"

버스터는 다시 생각했습니다. "짧아." 그가 결론을 내렸습니다.

"짧고 달콤하지." 아서가 말했습니다. "바로 시리얼처럼 말이야."

"나한테는 말이 되는데." 버스터가 말했습니다. "난 좋아. 그럼 지금 나와서 놀 수 있어?"

"나는 가사보다 더 많은 것이 필요해." 아서가 말했습니다. "나는 그것에 어울리는 선율이 필요해. 하지만 지금까지 그다지 운이 좋지 않아서..."

page 19

"흠." 버스터가 말했습니다. 그는 혼자 피아노에 앉아 있는 아서를 보았습니다. "아마도 넌 더 크게 생각해야 해."

"뭐가 더 큰 건데?"

"있잖아, 더 많은 사람, 더 많은 악기."

아서는 그 발상이 마음에 들었습니다.

"네가 더 많은 음악가와 있다면," 버스터가 계속했습니다. "선율을 만들어 내는 것이 쉬울 거야."

"더 많은 음악가?" 아서가 말했습니다. "네 말은 그러니까, 밴드 같은 거?"

"너 오디션도 보고 다 할 수 있잖아." 버스터가 말했습니다. "운동장을 살펴볼 수도 있지. 내가 장담하건대 많은 아이들이 흥미로워할 거야."

아서는 그의 코트를 잡았습니다. "좋아." 그가 말했습니다. "지금 찾아 보자."

page 20

학교 운동장은 뛰어다니며 소음을 만들고 있는, 옷을 잔뜩 껴입은 아이들로 가득 차 있었습니다.

"안녕, 프랜신!" 버스터가 말했습니다.

그녀는 떨어진 눈덩이 위에 서 있었습니다.

"아름다웠을 텐데." 그녀가 한숨 쉬었습니다.

"아서가 너한테 물어볼 것이 있대." 버스터가 말했습니다.

"다른 눈 조각상들을 모두 이길 눈 조각상. 그것은 용감했어. 그것은 대담했지."

"나 궁금한 게 있는데, 프랜신..." 아서가 시작했습니다.

"하지만 난 혼자서 할 수 없었어. 나는 친구들의 도움이 필요했어. 그리고 그들이 나를 위해 있어 주었나?" 그녀는 아서와 버스터를 올려다봤습니다. "아니, 대신 그들은 안에서 바보 같은 짓을 하고 있었지." 그녀는 팔짱을 끼었습니다. "난 그들을 용서할 수 있을 것 같지 않아."

"그것 참 안됐구나." 아서가 말했습니다. "가자, 버스터, 우리 이런 때에 그녀에게 물어볼 수 없어. 그녀가 너무 큰 고통에 빠져 있잖아."

page 22

"물어? 나한테 뭘 물어?"

"아서는 네가 밴드에 들어오면 좋겠대." 버스터가 말했습니다.

프랜신의 눈이 커졌습니다. "밴드? 내가 드럼을 치게 되는 거야?"

"그럴지도." 아서가 말했습니다. "하지만 네가 기분이 무척 나쁘다고 하니까..."

프랜신은 떨어진 눈덩이를 다시 보았습니다. 그녀는 그것을 발로 찼습니다. "뭐, 어때." 그녀가 말했습니다. "쉽게 얻은 것은, 쉽게 가는 거지." 그녀는 아서에게 몸을 돌렸습니다.

"그래서 우리 언제 시작해?"

4장

page 23

아서는 큰 콘서트장의 중앙으로 걸어 나오며 조명을 바라보았습니다. 비록 그는 보지 못해도, 관객들이 거기에 있다는 것을 알았습니다. 그들은 나라에서 가장 뛰어난 음악 비평가들이었습니다. 그들은 모두 그의 밴드가 크런치 시리얼 로고송을 연주하는 것을 들으러 왔습니다.

아서가 마이크에 대고 말했습니다. "신사 숙녀 여러분, 프로그램에 변경이 생겼습니다." 그가 공지했습니다. "보시다시피, 저는 아직 완전한 밴드를 갖추지 못했습니다. 하지만 버스터, 프랜신 그리고 제가 기꺼이—"

관객들은 야유하기 시작했습니다. 그들은 완전한 밴드가 연주하는 것을 들으러 나라 곳곳에서 날아왔지, 대충 끼워 맞춰진 몇몇 악기를 들으러 온 것이 아니었습니다.

page 24

"우리 시간을 낭비하지 마!"

"무대에서 내려와!"

"진짜 준비되면 오라고!"

아서가 손을 들었습니다. "제가 설명할 수 있다면..." 그가 시작했습니다.

"이봐, 아서!" 버스터가 말했습니다. "정신 차려!"

아서는 눈을 깜박였습니다. 그가 거실을 두리번거렸습니다. "나 정신 차리고 있지, 정신 차리고 있어." 그가 말했습니다.

"무슨 일이야?" 버스터가 물었습니다. "너 뭔가 걱정스러워하는 것 같아."

"음, 좀 그래. 만약 오늘 아무도 오지 않으면 어쩌지? 만약에 사람들이 오디션이 있다는 내 표지판을 무시하면 어떡하지?"

"음, 아서, 그게 문제가 될 것 같지는

않은데. 봐!"

리드 씨네 집 차고 밖으로, 아이들의 긴 줄이 형성되어 있었습니다. 그들은 각자 악기를 가지고 있었습니다.

page 25

"좋아!" 아서가 말했습니다. "시작해 보자."

버스터가 줄을 관리할 때, 리드 씨는 무슨 일이 일어나고 있는지 보러 나왔습니다.

버스터는 왜 아이들이 거기에 있는지 설명했습니다.

리드 씨는 안심한 것처럼 보였습니다. "아, 그 시리얼 일 때문에 그렇구나. 뭐, 이건 확실히 야심찬데." 그는 잠시 멈췄습니다. "우리가 모두를 먹여야 하니?"

"아, 아니에요." 버스터가 말했습니다. "아서가 전부 알아서 할 거예요."

차고 안에서, 아서는 크런치 시리얼을 몇 접시나 꺼내 두었습니다.

"먹어치워! 먹어치워!" 그가 말했습니다. "모두가 먹을 수 있을 만큼 충분히 있어."

몇 분간의 와그작거림이 있은 후, 오디션이 시작되었습니다.

수 엘렌이 맨 처음이었습니다. 그녀는 색소폰으로 몇 개의 음으로 된 악절을 연주했습니다.

page 26

"좋아." 아서가 말했습니다. "그런데 나 뭔가 달그락거리는 것을 들었는데?"

"내 생각에 크런치 시리얼이 내 악기에 들어간 것 같아."

"그래, 빼내도록 노력해 봐. 다음!"

아서는 아이들이 연주하는 밴조와 피콜로, 오보에 그리고 카주를 들었습니다. 한 아이는 트럼펫으로 너무 긴 음을 불어서 거의 기절할 뻔했습니다.

가장 압권은 도라 할머니가 도착했을 때였습니다.

"네 테스트에 대해 들었단다." 그녀가 말했습니다. "나를 특별 대우할 필요는 없다. 내가 몇 년 동안 구워준 쿠키에 대해서도 전혀 생각할 필요 없어. 그리고 치킨 스프에 대해서도 신경 쓰지 마. 그냥 들어 봐."

그리고 그 말과 함께, 그녀는 하모니카를 꺼내 연주하기 시작했습니다.

재즈의 음이 모두의 주목을 끌었습니다. 그리고 그녀는 노래했습니다. "할머니가 새 가방을 가졌네! 오늘 밤새도록 리듬에 맞춰..."

아서는 감명 받았습니다. "합격이에요!" 그가 말했습니다.

줄의 마지막에 있던 사람은 빙키 반스였습니다.

"준비됐어?" 그가 물었습니다.

아서가 고개를 끄덕였습니다.

"옛날에 죽은 어떤 사람이 쓴 클라리넷 독주야."

빙키는 복잡한 음들을 연주했습니다.

아서의 입이 떡 벌어졌습니다.

"와!" 버스터가 말했습니다. "아름다웠어!"

빙키가 그에게 성큼성큼 걸어왔습니다. "맞아, 맞아, 맞아… 그래서 나 합격이야 아니야?"

"당연하지!" 아서가 말했습니다. "음, 한 가지 조건하에…"

page 29

"그 조건은?"

"내가 크런치 마지막 상자를 끝내는 걸 네가 도와주는 것."

빙키가 미소 지었습니다. "좋아." 그가 말했습니다.

5장

page 30

아서는 새로 편성한 크런치 번치 밴드 앞에 섰습니다. 버스터와 프랜신 외에도, 빙키, 머피, 브레인, 수 엘렌, 프루넬라 그리고 도라 할머니가 멤버였습니다.

"*나*는 어디로 가야 해?" D.W.가 물었습니다.

그녀는 문가에 서 있었습니다.

아서는 그녀에게 걸어갔습니다. "오디션은 끝났어, D.W. 게다가, 넌 악기를 연주하지도 않잖아."

"걱정하지 마. 난 연주하고 싶지 않아. 난 단지 뭔가를 담당하고 싶어."

"모든 자리가 다 찼어." 아서가 단호하게 말했습니다. 그는 문을 열었습니다. "나딘이 널 부르는 것 같은데." 나딘은 D.W.의 보이지 않는 친구였습니다. "그녀가 눈 더미에 빠진 것 같아. 가서 확인해 보는 것이 좋을 거야."

page 31

"쳇!" D.W. 투덜거렸습니다. "오빠들은 꼭 두목 행세를 한다니까."

아서는 그녀 뒤로 문을 닫고 다른 사람들에게로 돌아왔습니다.

"자 이제, 우리 어디까지 했었지? 아, 맞아… 나는 큰 소리와 함께 시작하고 싶어. 그러니 모두들 정말 큰 음을 내야 해. 그럼 내가—"

"우리 이렇게 할—" 프랜신이 시작했습니다.

아서는 그녀를 쳐다보았습니다. "이보세요. 누가 질문이 있나요? 난 아무도 손드는 것을 보지 못했는데."

프랜신은 어이가 없어 눈을 굴리고 손을 들었습니다.

"그래, 프랜신?"

"내가 생각하기에 드럼롤로 시작하는 게 좋을 것 같아. 극적인 효과를 주기 위해서."

page 32

"맞아." 바이올린을 턱 아래에 대며

머피가 말했습니다. "그리고 현악기가 나오는 거지."

그녀는 연주하기 시작하자, 브레인이 첼로를 뜯기 시작했습니다.

"그러고 난 다음에 관악기를 더하는 거야." 수 엘렌이 말했습니다.

그녀는 프루넬라가 트럼펫을 드는 동안 색소폰을 불었습니다.

"아니야." 아서가 말했습니다.

다른 사람들은 계속 연주했습니다.

아서는 팔을 저었습니다. "아니야! 아니야! *아니야! 아니라고!*"

모두들 멈췄습니다. 귀가 먹먹할 정도의 정적이 흘렀습니다.

"내 얘기를 들어 봐." 아서가 말했습니다. "내가 참가 신청서를 가졌어. 내가 크런치를 15상자 먹었고, 이건 *나의* 로고송이야. 그러니 우리는 *내* 방식대로 연주할 거야! 질문 있는 사람?"

"없어."

"나는 없어."

"확실히 알아들었어."

page 34

"계속해."

아서는 심호흡을 했습니다. "좋아." 그가 말했습니다.

"하지만 우리 뭘 연주해?" 브레인이 물었습니다.

"내가 보여줄게." 아서가 말했습니다.

그는 악보를 나누어 주었습니다.

"여기 얼마 적혀 있지 않은데." 프랜신이 말했습니다. "음표 몇 개뿐이야."

"뭐, 로고송이니까." 아서가 말했습니다. "음이 반복돼. 이제, 모두 준비됐으면, 우리가 가진 모든 것을 쏟아부어 보자. 하나, 둘—"

아서는 연주를 시작하라고 몸짓했습니다.

그리고 그들이 시작했습니다.

뿌아앙!

이상한 소리가 차고에서 온 방향으로 퍼져나갔습니다.

그것은 티블 부인을 가장 먼저 덮쳤습니다. 그녀는 도보를 따라 걷고 있었습니다. 그 소리가 머리 위 나뭇가지에 쌓인 눈을 진동시켜, 마치 도넛에 뿌려진 가루 설탕처럼 그녀를 덮었습니다.

같은 시각, 미용사 밥은 팅글리 씨의 머리카락을 자르고 있었습니다.

뿌아앙!

그 소리는 닫힌 창문을 뚫고 울려 퍼졌습니다. 밥은 깜짝 놀랐고—그녀의 앞머리 대부분을 잘라버렸습니다.

그 소리는 마을 끝에서는 약해졌지만, 여전히 강력한 펀치를 날렸습니다. 머피의 부모님, 크로스와이어 부부는, 거실에서 그것을 들었습니다.

뿌아앙!

"공습이다." 에드 씨가 말했습니다.

"우리 공습 같은 거 없잖아요." 그의

부인 밀리센트 씨가 그에게 상기시켰습니다.

"글쎄, 나는 운에 맡기지 않아. 우리 공습 대피소에 돈을 많이 썼잖아. 우리 그걸 쓰는 게 좋을 거야."

그리고 그들 둘은 지하실—더 이상 들릴 것이 없는 곳으로 내려갔습니다.

6장

page 37

아서의 차고 안에서, 모두들 서로를 쳐다보았습니다. 그들의 입이 떡 벌어져 있었습니다.

"뭐," 아서가 말했습니다. "아마도 쾅 소리가 너무 컸나봐. 하지만 그래도 좋은 시작이라고 생각해."

차고 문을 노크하는 소리가 났습니다. 아서가 문을 열었습니다.

경찰관이 밖에 서 있었습니다. 그녀의 순찰차가 길에 있었습니다. 경광등이 번쩍이고 있었습니다.

"오, 이런." 아서가 말했습니다.

"불평 신고를 조사하고 있습니다." 경찰관이 말했습니다. "사실 여러 통의 전화를 받았어요."

page 38

"그래요?" 아서가 말했습니다. "뭐에 대해서요?"

경찰관은 노트를 봤습니다. "어떤 사람은 고양이가 고문당하는 것 같다고 생각했습니다. 여기 와 보니 그런 것 같지는 않군요. 고양이가 있습니까?"

"고양이는 없어요." 아서가 말했습니다. "단지 개가 한 마리 있어요. 그리고 그는 멀쩡해요. 진짜예요."

"다른 어떤 사람은 방사능 유출을 경고하는 사이렌을 들었다고 합니다." 경찰관은 아서의 어깨 너머를 봤습니다. "허가되지 않은 물질을 여기에서 사용하고 있는 것은 아니겠죠? 우라늄은 없나요? 그 비슷한 것이라도?"

아서는 고개를 저었습니다. "우리는 단지 로고송을 연습하고 있었어요."

경찰관은 밴드의 멤버들을 훑어보았습니다. "알겠습니다, 그럼." 그녀는 노트를 치웠습니다. "모두 적법한 것 같군요. 하지만 충고 하나만 할게요..."

page 39

"네, 경관님."

"소리를 낮춰요. 로고송이 *쨍그랑*거리게 하지 마세요—무슨 말인지 알겠죠."

아서는 고개를 끄덕였습니다. "네 알아요, 경관님. 감사합니다, 경관님. 안녕히 가세요."

그는 그녀 뒤로 문을 닫았습니다.

"아슬아슬했어." 버스터가 말했습니다.

빙키는 창밖을 보았습니다. "그녀가

경광등을 껐어. 유감이네. 그래도, 우리 이번 주에 신문에 나올 수 있겠다."

아서가 모두에게로 몸을 돌렸습니다. 모두들 짐을 싸고 있었습니다.

"이봐! 기다려! 뭐하는 거야? 우리 음을 맞춰야지! 포기하지 마!"

"우리는 체포되고 싶지 않아." 수 엘렌이 말했습니다.

"그리고 난 매우 바빠. 난 내 일정표에 감옥 시간을 만들지 않을 거야." 머피가 말했습니다.

"하지만 콘테스트가..."

page 40

브레인이 첼로를 들고 옆으로 움직이며 아서를 피해 지나갔습니다.

"우리 모두 점심 먹으러 집에 가는 거야." 프루넬라가 말했습니다.

프랜신이 그를 보았습니다. "우리 나중에 돌아올 거야. 우리가 간 사이에 네가 영감을 받으면 좋겠다."

"*아주 많이* 영감 받았으면 좋겠어." 머피가 덧붙였습니다.

도라 할머니는 코트를 입었습니다. "너무 낙담하지 마라, 얘야. 아직까진 듣기 거북하지만, 난 네가 그걸 고칠 수 있다고 믿는단다."

밴드의 나머지는 줄을 지어 나갔습니다.

아서는 그들이 떠나는 것을 보았습니다. 오직 버스터만이 남았습니다.

"너 점심 먹으면 기분이 나아질 거야." 그가 말했습니다. "난 언제나 배가 가득 차면 더 잘 생각하거든."

아서의 배는 긴장감으로 가득했습니다.

"나 지금 음식에 대해 생각할 수 없어. 난 할 일이 있어."

그는 집을 향해 움직였습니다.

page 42

"너 잠시 휴식을 취해야 해, 그래도." 버스터가 말했습니다.

아서는 몸을 홱 돌렸습니다.

"모차르트가 휴식을 취했을까?"

버스터는 알 수 없었습니다. 버스터는 모차르트의 일과에 대해서 말할 수 있기는커녕, 모차르트의 철자도 쓰지 못했습니다.

"'둥글게 둥글게'를 쓴 사람이 휴식을 취했을까? 내 생각에는 아니야. 그들은 헌신적이었어. 그들은 전념했어. 그리고 나도 그래."

7장

page 43

아서 뱃속의 긴장감은 사라지지 않았습니다. 그것은 그곳에서 단단하고 불편하게 계속 자리 잡고 있었습니다. 아서는 그것을 무시하려고 했습니다. 그는 거실에 있는 피아노 앞에 등을 구부리고 앉아 있었습니다. 그는 건반을 쳐다보았습니다.

건반이 그를 마주 바라보는 것 같았습니다.

아서가 한 음을 쳤습니다.

딩.

아서는 다른 음을 치고 싶었습니다. 하지만 그는 망설였습니다. 한 음을 고르기엔 너무 많은 음들이 있었습니다.

"크런치를 먹어요." 아서가 노래했습니다. 그는 끙끙댔습니다. "좋아, 하지만 충분하지 않아. 난 절대 더 좋은 것을 떠올리지 못할 거야."

page 44

그의 머리가 건반 위로 떨어지며, 뒤죽박죽 섞인 화음이 공기를 채우게 했습니다.

눈을 감으니 어두웠습니다. 그가 천천히 눈을 떴습니다. 그는 어둠 속에서 겨우 볼 수 있었습니다.

안개가 앞쪽에서 갈라지며, 삐걱거리는 다리를 드러냈습니다. 그것은 밧줄과 나무판자로 매어 있었습니다. 판자는 흰색과 검은색으로—마치 피아노의 건반처럼 칠해져 있었습니다. 그것은 바람에 천천히 흔들리고 있었습니다.

저 다리는 안전해 보이지 않아, 아서가 생각했습니다. 하지만 그것이 산길로 가는 유일한 방법이었습니다.

D.W.가 건너편에 서 있었습니다.

"만약 안전하게 건너고 싶다면," 그녀가 말했습니다. "오빠는 올바른 음을 연주해야만 해."

"알았어." 아서가 말했습니다. "하지만 올바른 음이 뭔데?"

그의 여동생은 웃음을 터뜨렸습니다. "오빠가 찾게 될 거야." 그녀가 말했습니다. "어떻게 해서든 말이야."

page 45

아서는 얼굴을 찌푸렸습니다. 그는 앞으로 뛰어서, 세 번째 판자에 내렸습니다.

동!

"그게 아서 오빠를 위한 작은 한 발걸음이네." D.W.가 말했습니다. "계속해."

아서는 검은 판자 위로 뛰었습니다.

딩!

"두 번 다 성공." D.W.가 말했습니다.

아서의 기분이 나아졌습니다. 아마도 이것은 그렇게 어렵지 않을지도 모릅니다. 그는 바로 옆 판자로 걸어갔습니다.

삐걱!

오 이런, 아서가 생각했습니다.

그가 다리에서 떨어질 때, D.W.가 흥얼대는 것을 들었습니다. 어째서 그녀는 좀 더 일찍 그 선율을 흥얼대지 않았던 것일까요? 그것은 기억하기 쉬웠습니다. 그것은 좋은 박자를 가지고 있었습니다. 그는 다리를 건너면서 제대로 연주

할 수도 있었습니다.

아서는 머리를 불쑥 일으켜 세웠습니다. 다리는 사라졌습니다. 산길도 그랬습니다. 그는 다시 피아노를 마주 보고 있었습니다.

page 46

하지만 D.W.는 여전히 흥얼대고 있었습니다.

아서는 그 소리를 따라 복도로 갔습니다. 그것은 위층에서 들려오고 있었습니다.

아서는 발끝으로 살금살금 계단을 올라 D.W.의 방으로 갔습니다. 그는 안을 살짝 보았습니다.

그의 여동생이 침대 위에 앉아, 나딘의 머리를 빗고 있었습니다. 비록 그가 나딘을 볼 수 없어도 아서는 그렇다는 것을 알 수 있었습니다. 오로지 D.W.만이 그녀를 볼 수 있었습니다.

D.W.는 빗질을 하면서, 노래를 부르기 시작했습니다.

"오, 나는 예감이 드네
아침, 저녁 그리고 점심
모두 씹기 재미있을 거라고,
내가 그걸 나딘과 함께 한다면!"

그것은 이전에 흥얼거렸던 것과 같은 노래였습니다. 다만 그녀가 가사를 덧붙였을 뿐입니다.

아서의 눈이 툭 튀어나왔습니다. 그것은 줄곧 바로 그의 앞에 있었습니다. 그가 해야 할 전부는 나딘이 나오는 부분을 바꾸는 것뿐이었습니다.

page 48

"완벽해! 정말 완벽해!"

그는 아래층으로 뛰어 내려갔습니다.

D.W.는 아서가 서 있었던 자리를 보았습니다.

"그거 아서 오빠였어?" 나딘이 물었습니다.

"그런 것 같아."

"오빠는 정신이 나간 것이 틀림없어." 나딘이 말했습니다. "그 시리얼을 너무 많이 먹어서. 그거 이름이 뭐랬지?"

"크런치." D.W.가 말했습니다.

"만약 나한테 묻는다면," 나딘이 말했습니다. "그는 정신 나갈 때까지 와그작거릴 거야."

둘은 모두 웃었습니다.

8장

page 49

밴드 멤버들이 점심을 먹고 돌아왔을 때 아서의 차고 안 분위기는 어두웠습니다. 해는 밖에서 비추고 있었지만, 차고는 구름에 가려 어두운 것 같았습니다.

프랜신은 드럼으로 느린 행진곡을 두

드리고 있었습니다.

머피는 바이올린으로 듣기 괴로운 끼익 소리를 내며 준비를 하고 있었습니다. 그것은 마치 그녀가 실수로 고양이의 꼬리를 밟았을 때 나는 소리 같았습니다.

빙키는 클라리넷에 새로운 리드를 달고 있었습니다. "다들 점심을 많이 먹었길 바라." 그가 말했습니다. "나는 그랬어. 긴 오후가 될 것 같거든."

page 50

심지어 도라 할머니조차 조금 우울한 것 같았습니다. 그녀는 발을 구르며 혼자 노래를 부르고 있었습니다.

"시간은 빠르게 지나가고,
아서는 제자리에 있고,
그는 모든 의문을 치워 버려야 하지.
그리고 우리에게 그가 가진 걸 보여줘야해."

각 행마다, 그녀는 부드럽게 하모니카를 불었습니다.

"힘내, 모두들." 버스터가 말했습니다. "난 아서가 우리를 실망시키지 않을 것이라고 확신해."

"그는 그러고 싶지 않을지도 모르지." 프루넬라가 말했습니다. "하지만 그렇게 많은 크런치 시리얼을 먹은 것이 그의 뇌를 썩게 했을지도 몰라."

프랜신은 얼굴을 찌푸렸습니다. "만약 그게 그의 귀에서 흘러나온다면, 난 여기서 빠질래."

page 51

바로 그때 아서가 서둘러 들어왔습니다. 그의 뇌는 적어도 겉으로 보기엔 썩은 것 같지 않았습니다. 사실, 그는 매우 기뻐 보였습니다.

"내가 찾았어, 모두들! 내가 로고송을 찾았어. 들어 봐!"

방안이 조용해졌습니다.

아서는 노래 부르기 시작했습니다.

"오, 나는 예감이 드네
아침, 저녁 그리고 점심
모두 씹기 재미있을 거라고,
내가 그걸... 크런치와 함께 한다면!"

"정말 좋은 박자를 가졌는데." 도라 할머니가 손가락으로 딱 소리를 내며 말했습니다. "그리고 넌 거기에 맞춰 춤을 출 수 있겠어."

버스터는 박수를 쳤습니다. "잘했어, 아서!"

"놀라워!" 프랜신이 말했습니다. "그건 정말로 정말로..."

page 53

"좋아." 머피가 그녀 대신 마무리했습니다.

"뭐가 너에게 영감을 줬니?" 브레인이

물었습니다.

"영감에 대해 설명하기는 어려워." 아서가 말했습니다. "난 거실에 앉아 있었어. 그리고 이 선율을 들었..."

아서는 잠시 멈췄습니다. 그는 갑자기 그의 영감이 어디서 왔었는지 기억했습니다. 그는 눈을 내리깔고 안경을 만지작거렸습니다.

"나, 어, 이 선율을 내 머릿속에서 들었어. 그리고... 그리고 가사가 나에게 왔어. 그게 다야."

버스터는 감명 받았습니다. "와! 위대한 로고송은 그렇게 탄생하는 것 같아. 처음에는 아무것도 없다가... 두 번째도 아무것도 없어. 그러고 나서, 휙! 어디선지 모르게—갑자기 아름다운 것이 나오는 거야."

"그런가 봐." 수 엘렌이 말했습니다.

"나는 더 안 좋은 경우도 들었던 것 같은데." 빙키가 말했습니다.

"잘됐다, 아서." 도라 할머니가 말했습니다.

아서는 입술을 깨물었습니다. "뭐, 모두가 좋아한다니 기뻐. 이제 우리 각자 부분을 연주할 차례야."

page 54

그는 악보를 나누어 주었습니다.

"우리 모두 함께 이걸 연주하고 노래 부를 수 있어." 그는 활짝 웃었습니다. "그리고 뭔가 추가하고 싶다면, 바로 시작해 봐."

그들은 몇 분 동안 연습했습니다. 모두들 매우 편안해 보였습니다.

아서는 녹음기를 준비했습니다.

"준비됐어?" 그가 물었습니다.

모두들 고개를 끄덕였습니다.

아서는 녹음 버튼을 눌렀습니다.

그들은 곡을 끝까지 다 연주를 했습니다—하지만 너무 시끄럽지 않게요. 아서는 눈을 감고서 크고 힘차게 노래 불렀습니다. 그가 눈을 떴을 때, 그는 강아지 팔이 마당에서 위아래로 뛰어오르고 있는 것을 알아차렸습니다.

이것은 좋은 징조야, 그가 생각했습니다.

9장

page 55

테이프가 준비되자, 아서는 얼른 우편을 보내고 싶었습니다. 그는 좋은 소식을 듣자마자 알려 주겠다는 약속과 함께 밴드 멤버들을 집으로 보냈습니다.

"우린 부자가 될 거야!" 버스터가 말했습니다.

아서는 고개를 저었습니다. "음, 버스터, 상에는 상금이 포함되어 있지 않아."

"오, 그래, 그럼 우린 유명해질 거야. 난 융통성 있어."

그는 그의 튜바를 두 번 빵 하고 불고 집으로 향했습니다.

아서는 우편물을 준비하려고 집 안으로 들어갔습니다. 그는 재빨리 편지를 써서 봉투 안에 테이프와 함께 넣었습니다. 도라 할머니가 우표를 얼마나 많이 붙여야 할지 도와주었습니다.

page 56

그리고 그는 다시 밖으로 나왔습니다.

"어디가, 아서 오빠?" D.W.가 물었습니다.

그녀와 나딘은 눈 속에서 놀고 있었습니다.

"지금 말 못해, D.W. 난 바빠."

그의 여동생은 그의 팔 아래에 있는 우편물을 발견했습니다. "오! 그게 콘테스트용 로고송이야? 나 오빠가 뭔가 연주하는 것을 들었어."

아서는 우편물을 내려다보았습니다.

"이거? 어, 그래, 그런 것 같아."

"그래서, 오빠 뭘 떠올렸어? 들어 보자."

"너 공손하게 굴 필요 없어, D.W. 난 너랑 나딘이 관심 없다는 것을 알아."

"나딘은 하지도 않은 말을 했다고 하는 걸 좋아하지 않아, 아서 오빠. 나딘은 스스로 결정하는 것을 좋아해."

page 57

"걔한테 잘 됐네." 아서가 말했습니다. "하지만, 정말로, 나는 바쁘—"

D.W.가 얼굴을 찌푸렸습니다. "오빠 그 노래를 좋아하는 거 맞지?"

"오, 그럼. 아주 많이."

"그럼, 나한테 노래해 봐."

"오... 씹기... 와그작거리기... 딱, 탁 탁, 펑... 그런 거야. 이런, 시간 좀 봐. 난 마지막 우편 수거를 놓치면 안 돼."

D.W.는 뭔가 더 말을 하려고 했지만, 아서는 더 이상 듣지 않고 가버렸습니다.

D.W.는 나딘에게 몸을 돌렸습니다. 가끔씩 그녀의 오빠는 상당히 이상했습니다. 그녀는 그게 전염되는 것이 아니길 바라면서, 어깨를 으쓱했습니다.

아서는 길을 따라 가면서, 속도를 줄여 보통 걸음으로 걸었습니다. 그는 D.W.에게 로고송이 어디서 나온 것이었는지 말하는 걸 피했습니다. 물론, 그녀는 그녀가 그를 도왔었다는 사실조차 몰랐습니다. 그러므로 그녀에게 말해야 할 이유는 없었습니다. 꼭 그럴 이유는 없었죠. 위대한 예술가들은 언제나 주위 사람과 장소에서 영감을 얻는 법이었습니다.

page 58

아서는 공원에 설치된 콘서트 무대 위에 있었습니다. 그는 피아노 앞에 앉아 있었습니다. 뒤로는 환호하는 관중들 소리를 들을 수 있었습니다. 그는 로고송의 테마를 연주하고 큰 미소를 지어 보였습니다. 관중들은 환호했습니다.

여러 줄 뒤편에서 D.W.가 무대 앞으로 나오고 있었습니다.

"아서 오빠! 아서 오빠! 나 그 노래 알아! 오빠 사람들한테 진실을 말했어?"

아서는 그의 여동생의 목소리를 들었지만 그녀를 보지 못했습니다.

"D.W., 어디 있니?"

D.W.는 거의 무대에 닿았었지만, 그녀가 계단을 오르기 전에, 몇몇 사람들이 서둘러 앞으로 나와 그녀의 길을 막았습니다.

page 60

"방금 누구였습니까?" 우람한 경호팀의 책임자가 물었습니다.

"오, 그냥 내 팬 중 한 명이에요." 아서가 말했습니다. "몇몇은 매우 완강하죠."

아서는 한숨 쉬었습니다. 그는 우체통에 도착했었습니다. 그가 해야 하는 일의 전부는 봉투를 넣는 것이었습니다. 그냥 손잡이를 내려서, 안에 떨어뜨리기만 하면 됐습니다. 아주 쉬운 일이었습니다, 정말로요. 하지만 어째서인지 그는 그렇게 할 수 없었습니다, 아직은 말이죠. 그는 단지 거기에 서서, 햇살에 눈을 깜박이고 있었습니다.

10장

page 61

2주 후 토요일 아침, D.W.와 아서는 잠옷을 입고 TV를 보고 있었습니다.

"바이오닉 버니가 캡틴 정크 푸드를 무찌를 수 있을까요? 광고 후에 알아봅시다."

"캡틴 정크 푸드는 꽤 강력해." D.W.가 말했습니다. "내 생각엔 바이오닉 버니는 여유가 없을 거야."

"그럴지도." 아서가 말했습니다. "그리고 저 방송은 나를 배고프게 만들어."

그는 부엌으로 향했습니다—하지만 TV에서 어떤 노래가 나오자 갑자기 멈췄습니다.

page 62

"오, 나는 예감이 드네
아침, 저녁 그리고 점심..."

아서는 몸을 돌려 턱시도를 입은 크런치 너겟이 마이크 앞에서 노래 부르고 있는 것을 보았습니다.

"모두 씹기 재미있을 거라고
내가 그걸... 크런치와 함께 한다면!"

D.W.는 하품했습니다. "이 광고 옛날 것만큼 좋지 않아—이봐, 잠깐만..."

아서는 TV로 뛰어가서 그 앞에 섰습니다.

"D.W., 내가 설명할 수 있어."

그의 여동생은 팔짱을 끼었습니다. "그러는 게 좋을 거야." 그녀가 말했습니다.

page 63

"거기 진정 좀 해라." 아빠가 부엌에서 머리를 내밀며 말했습니다. "아침식사가 준비됐어. 내 특제 오트밀이야. 섬유질이 그 중간 이름이지."

D.W.는 TV를 끄고 부엌으로 향했습니다. 아서가 따라갔습니다.

테이블에는 아주 단단한 오트밀이 담긴 그릇으로 준비되어 있었습니다.

"그러니까," 아서가 말했습니다. "내가 말하려고 하고 있었어. 내 말은, 처음에는 아니었어. 하지만 난 그 응모권을 절대 보내지 않았어. 그러다가 다시 보냈지. 하지만 여전히 너한테 말하지 않았고... 난 내가 질 거라고—그러니까, 네가 질 거라고 확신했어."

D.W.는 어이가 없어서 눈을 굴렸습니다. "아서 오빠, 오빤 평소보다도 더 말이 안 되는 소리를 하네. 무슨 일이야?"

"너희들은 이걸 좋아할 거야." 리드 씨가 말했습니다. "한 접시면—너희들은 저녁 때까지 배고프지 않을 거야."

그는 오트밀을 숟가락으로 두드렸습니다.

page 64

"사실, 너희는 저녁 때까지 움직이지 못할지도 몰라."

"그 콘테스트!" 아서가 계속했습니다. "너한테 말하지 않은 건 왜냐하면—"

"나한테 뭘 말해?"

"그러니까 내가—"

그는 초인종 소리에 방해받았습니다.

"누가 왔을까?" 리드 씨가 말했습니다.

그는 앞문으로 가서 문을 열었습니다. 배달원이 밖에 서 있었습니다. 그는 시리얼이 담긴 접시 같이 생긴 모자를 쓰고 있었습니다.

"여기가 리드 가족 거주지인가요?"

"그런데요?" 리드 씨가 조심스럽게 말했습니다.

그 남자는 목을 가다듬었습니다. "크런치 시리얼 회사를 대신해서, 당신께 1년 치 시리얼을 선물하게 되어 기쁩니다."

그는 시리얼 상자가 들어 있는 큰 짐짝을 리드 씨네 집 진입로에 내려놓은 그의 파트너에게 몸짓으로 신호를 보냈습니다.

"또한 여기 크런치 시리얼 로고송 콘테스트의 우승자라는 것을 알리는 증서가 여기 있습니다."

page 65

리드 씨는 어쩔 줄 몰라 하는 것 같았습니다. "그럼 그건 누구에게 주는 거죠?"

"D.W. 리드 양에게요."

"나요?" D.W.가 말했습니다.

아서가 한숨 쉬었습니다. "그게 내가 너한테 얘기하려고 했던 거야."

잠시 후, 온 가족이 밖에 모였습니다.

"너한테 내가 너의 노래를 보냈다고 말하고 싶었어." 아서가 말했습니다. "하지만 네가 희망을 너무 크게 가지길 원하진 않았어. 너 화난 거 아니지?"

D.W.는 단지 웃었습니다. "오빠가 그 형편없는 걸 보냈다고? 그리고 그게 우승했어?" 그녀는 활짝 웃었습니다. "물론, 난 그것보다 더 좋은 노래가 있는데!"

"어, 정말?" 아서가 말했습니다. "예를 들면?"

D.W.는 미소를 지었습니다. "뭐, 오늘 아침에 내가 쓴 노래도 있어.

오, 모두들 생각하죠
내 오빠가 냄새난다고
노란색 치즈 조각 같이!
하지만 난, 난 말하죠
그는 괜찮다고
산들바람이 부는 한."

page 67

"D.W.!"

그의 여동생은 뛰기 시작했습니다. 아서는 뒤에서 그녀를 쫓았습니다.

"돌아와." 그가 말했습니다. "내가 누가 냄새나는지 보여주지. 그래도 시리얼을 밟지는 마."

"엄마아."

"아빠아!"

부모님은 한숨 쉬었습니다.

"누가 이 모든 시리얼을 다 먹지?" 리드 씨가 물었습니다.

리드 부인은 이제 서로에게 눈덩이를 던지고 있는 아서와 D.W.를 가리켰습니다. "*재네*들이 먹을 거예요. 안 보여요? 지금 식욕을 돋우고 있잖아요."

"오." 리드 씨가 말했습니다. "그런 경우라면, 그렇게 하게 내버려 둡시다."

그리고 두 사람은 그들 뒤로 문을 굳게 닫으며, 실내로 돌아갔습니다.

Chapter 1

1. B "Yes, siree, on a chilly morning like this, everyone needs some oatmeal that will really stick to your ribs."

2. D He tilted the pot and tried to spoon some into her bowl. But nothing came out. The oatmeal had hardened like cement.

3. C His father shook his head. "I don't understand the appeal of that sugar-coated cardboard. Believe me, all you'll get from that stuff is a mouthful of cavities."

4. A Arthur opened the envelope and read the note inside aloud. *"Welcome to the Crunch Cereal Jingle Contest. Send us your song—and you could win a year's supply of Crunch cereal."*

5. C "There's something here in the small print," said Arthur. "Include twenty boxtops with each entry." He sighed. "That's a lot of crunching."

Chapter 2

1. A Over the next few days, Arthur thought about jingles while brushing his teeth.

2. D "Sometimes, it' s good to take a break," said Mrs. Read. "Recharge your creative batteries. Clear your head. Why don't you go make a snowman?"

3. C The snowball was beginning to look like a giant piece of Crunch cereal. " Is that what 1 think it is?"

4. "We've been over this, D.W. You have your job." "I know, I know. I'm supposed to eat the cereal."

5. Arthur looked up at the sky and sighed. Why couldn't inspiration hit him like a flash of lightning? He was ready. He was waiting.

Chapter 3

1. C The school music room was empty except for Arthur. All the other kids were out at recess, running around and playing in the snow. Arthur was trying out notes at the piano.

2. B Arthur cleared his throat. "Eat Crunch," he said.

3. C "What would be bigger?" "You know, more people, more instruments."

4. A "But 1 couldn't do it by myself. I needed the help of my friends. And were they here for me?" She looked up at Arthur and Buster. "No, they were inside doing some dumb thing instead." She folded her arms. "I don't think I'll ever be able to forgive them."

5. D Francine looked back at the fallen pile of snow. She gave it a kick. "Oh, well," she said. "Easy come, easy go." She turned back to Arthur. "So, when do we start?"

Chapter 4

1. B *The audience started to boo. They had flown in from all over the country to hear the full band, not a few instruments patched together.*

2. D " Well, I am, a little. What if nobody comes today? What if they just ignored my signs about auditioning?" "Um, Arthur, I don't think that will be a problem. Look!" Outside the Read garage, a long line of kids had formed. Each of them was holdìng an instrument.

3. A Inside the garage, Arthur had put out bowls of Crunch cereal.

4. D And with that, she pulled out a harmonica and began to play.

5. C "That you he1p me finish the last box of Crunch." Binky smiled. "It's a deal," he said.

Chapter 5

1. A Arthur stood in front of the newly formed Crunch Bunch band. Besides Buster and Francine, it included Binky, Muffy, the Brain, Sue Ellen, Prunella, and Grandrna Thora.

2. B "Don't worry. I don't want to play. I just want to be in charge."

3. B "Listen to me," said Arthur. "I got the entry form. I've eaten fifteen boxes of Crunch, and this is *my* jingle. So we're going to play it *my* way! Any questions?"

4. C "But what do we play from?" asked the Brain. "I'll show you," said Arthur. He passed out some sheet music.

5. D The sound shook the snow from the branches overhead, covering her like powdered sugar on a doughnut. At the same time, Bob the barber was cutting Miss Tingley's hair. *WHRAMMMPAARROOOOO!* The sound blasted through the closed windows. Bob was startled—and clipped off most of her bangs. The sound weakened at the edge of town, but it still packed a punch. Muffy's parents, the Crosswires, heard it in their living room. *Whrammmmmpaarrooooo!* "It's an air raid," said Ed.

Chapter 6

1. C "I'm investigating a complaint," said the officer. "Actually, we had a number of calls."

2. C "Keep the volume down. Try not to let your jingle *jangle*—if you know what I mean."

3. B "We're all going home for lunch," said Prunella. Francine looked at him. "We'll come back later. I just hope you're inspired while we're gone."

4. A "You'll feel better after lunch," he said. "I know I always think better on a full stomach."

5. D "Did the guy who wrote 'Ring-Around-the-Rose' take breaks? I don't think so. They were dedicated. They were committed. And so am I."

Chapter 7

1. B He sat in his living room hunched over the piano. He stared at the keys.

2. A *The fog parted up ahead, revealing a creaky bridge. It was strung with rope and wooden planks. The planks were painted white and black—like the keys of a piano. They swayed in the wind.*

3. D *D.W. was standing on the other side. "If you want to cross safely," she said, "you have to play the right notes."*

4. A "Perfect! Just PERFECT!"

5. C Arthur's eyes bulged. It was all there right in front of him. All he had to do was change the Nadine part.

Chapter 8

1. D "He might not want to," said Prunella. "But eating all that Crunch cereal may have rotted his brain."

2. C "I, uh, heard this tune in my head. And then . . . and then the words just came to me. That's all."

3. A Arthur bit his lip. "Well, I'm glad everyone likes it. Now we just have to play our parts."

4. B Arthur set up his tape recorder. "Ready?" he asked. Everyone nodded. Arthur pushed the record button.

5. A When he opened his eyes, he noticed Pal jumping up and down in the yard. It was a good sign, he thought.

Chapter 9

1. B Once the tape was ready, Arthur couldn't wait to get it into the mail. He sent the band home with his promise to let everyone know as soon as he heard anything.

2. A "So, what did you come up with? Let's hear it."

3. C So there was no reason to tell her. Not really. Great artists were always taking inspiration from the people and places around them.

4. D *D.W. had almost reached the stage, but before she could climb the stairs, several people rushed forward to block her way.*

5. B He had arrived at the mailbox. All he had to do was drop in the envelope. Just pull down the handle, and drop it in. Nothing to it, really. But somehow he couldn't. Not yet. He just stood there, blinking in the sunlight.

Chapter 10

1. A On Saturday morning two weeks later, D.W. and Arthur were watching

TV in their pajamas.

2. D " D.W., I can explain everything." His sister folded her arms. "You better," she said.

3. B He went to the front door and opened it. A delivery man stood outside. He was wearing a hat shaped like a bowl of cereal.

4. C "We also have a certificate proclaiming the winner of the Crunch Cereal Jingle Contest." Mr. Read looked overwhelmed. "And that is?" "Ms. D.W. Read."

5. D Mrs. Read pointed to Arthur and D.W., who were now pelting each other with snowballs. "They will. Don't you see? They're working on their appetites." "Oh," said Mr. Read. "In that case, let's leave them to it."